Praise for

Winning Him Without Words

Moving. Challenging. Full of devastating, healing truth. No two
ways about it: Dineen Miller and Lynn Donovan have crafted a mas-
terpiece in *Winning Him Without Words*. For those who've felt alone
in the battle to win their husbands to Christ, help is here! In fact,
any marriage—even those, like mine, in which spouses share a faith
in Jesus—would be strengthened and blessed by putting the 10 keys
in this book into practice. Wives, the time is now. Take the truths
these two women share and let them infuse your marriage with
what we all desire: God's amazing love and blessing.

Karen Ball
Editor and bestselling novelist of *The Breaking Point* and the Family Honor series

I am the daughter of a brave mother who was married to an unbeliever. My mother's decision to follow Jesus even if my dad didn't
made all the difference to me as a little girl and propelled me into
Christian leadership as an adult. I am forever grateful for women
like Lynn and Dineen who live out a message of "God is enough."
Winning Him Without Words is a lifeline of hope and help for any
woman who is struggling in a spiritually mismatched marriage.

Pam Farrel
Relationship specialist, international speaker, and author of more than 30
books, including the bestselling *Men Are Like Waffles, Women Are Like Spaghetti*

For anyone who endures a spiritually mismatched marriage—hoping and praying that things might improve—here's authentic help
from two women who know this topic from the inside out. Never
preachy or harsh, these authors reveal their own struggles and difficulties as wives caught up in spiritually mismatched marriages.
Winning Him Without Words is a must-read for hurting wives as they
prayerfully seek change in their husbands and meaningful transformation in their marriages.

Dr. David and Lisa Frisbie
The Center for Marriage and Family Studies, Del Mar, California
Authors of *Becoming Your Husband's Best Friend* and other books

C.S. Lewis once said that friendship is born at that moment one person says to another, "What! You too? I thought I was the only one." That's what *Winning Him Without Words* is like. For the woman who is married to a man who doesn't share her faith in Christ, this book is a faithful friend who will encourage her in her feelings of aloneness, anxiety, frustration (and all the other emotions that come with living in a spiritually mismatched marriage) and point her to the One who can and will make something good out of them. This book will give great hope to those who may wonder if thriving is out of reach.

Nancy Kennedy
Author of *When He Doesn't Believe*

As a "marriage" author, whenever I have a reader or audience member ask me, "What should I do if my husband isn't a believer?" I have felt inadequate to support him or her. Now I have a new approach—pray and hand the person this book. As I read through these pages, I was humbled by the wisdom and encouragement that these women share—much of which was a timely reminder for my own marriage. With honest struggle and authentic hope, Dineen and Lynn show women how to make God the very center of their unequal marriages.

Kathi Lipp
Author of *The Husband Project* and *The Marriage Project*

It has been a wonderful gift and blessing to "meet" Dineen and Lynn through their journeys. As one who is also unequally yoked in a spiritually mismatched marriage (to a wonderful guy, for 29 years!), the relief in knowing I am not alone is huge. That, coupled with practical keys they share as they share of themselves, has invigorated our marriage and brought honor to God.

Kathy Pride
Author of *What the Bible Is All About for Moms*

LYNN DONOVAN
& DINEEN MILLER

winning him
without **words**

Regal

From Gospel Light
Ventura, California, U.S.A.

Published by Regal
From Gospel Light
Ventura, California, U.S.A.
www.regalbooks.com
Printed in the U.S.A.

Library of Congress Cataloging-in-Publication Data
Donovan, Lynn.
Winning him without words : 10 keys to thriving in your spiritually mismatched
marriage / Lynn Donovan, Dineen Miller.
p. cm.
Includes bibliographical references (p.).
ISBN 978-0-8307-5605-6 (trade paper)
1. Wives—Religious life. 2. Christian women—Family relationships. 3. Husbands—
Religious life. 4. Non-church-affiliated people—Family relationships. 5. Marriage—
Religious aspects—Christianity. 6. Interfaith marriage. I. Miller, Dineen. II. Title.
BV4528.15.D66 2010
248.8'44—dc22
2010035106

Rights for publishing this book outside the U.S.A. or in non-English languages are
administered by Gospel Light Worldwide, an international not-for-profit ministry.
For additional information, please visit www.glww.org, email info@glww.org, or write
to Gospel Light Worldwide, 1957 Eastman Avenue, Ventura, CA 93003, U.S.A.

To order copies of this book and other Regal products in bulk quantities,
please contact us at 1-800-446-7735.

To the Lord Jesus Christ and to our Mikes

Contents

Acknowledgments

We would like to thank our editor, Kim Bangs; Elizabeth Wingate, our copyeditor; Mark Weising, the managing editor; and the entire Regal team for believing in our message and following God's leading on this amazing journey. We are still in awe of all God has done.

Lynn Would Like to Thank . . .

My husband and my best friend, Mike, who encourages me in my every endeavor. I love you with a full heart.

My daughter, Caitie, who believes in me and puts up with my harebrained humor. Thank you for always supporting me and reading my drafts. I love you, girl.

My son and Fantasy Football partner, Brad. Go Pink Princesses. Love you, son.

My friends from Sunridge who always gave me words of encouragement and prayed often over this book; and my pastor, Greg Sidders, much of whose wisdom can be found in these pages.

My mom, Sue Parks, and dad, Vern Ratzlaff, and sister, Kayla Arnesen, who know me well and love me anyway.

My online friends and online community who encouraged me. I can't even begin to name all of you who helped make this book possible because of your prayers. You know who you are and I am hugging you.

Especially, I want to thank each and every one of you who pray for my husband's salvation. You are a priceless gem.

Dineen Would Like to Thank . . .

My wonderful husband, Mike, for always supporting and encouraging me in my pursuits, whatever they may be. I adore you.

My parents, Donna and James Marco, for always believing in me and loving me like parents should. My precious daughters, Rachel and Leslie, for believing in Mom too.

My amazing critique partners and best friends—Ronie Kendig, Robin Miller and Heather Diane Tipton—for always being there, even when I crossed the realm from fiction to nonfiction. These are the most amazing women you will ever meet—or read.

The sweet group of unequally yoked ladies in Zürich, Switzerland, for taking me into their 1Peter3 group and encouraging me in the beginning of my journey.

The San Jose Christian Writers, for their prayers and encouragement.

Camy Tang, for being part of the process God used to bring Lynn and me together, for her great tea and scones, and for her constant support.

And special thanks to all who have prayed for this ministry, our book and my family, especially my daughter during her surgeries and recovery, and for my precious hubby. I can't wait to hug you all in heaven!

We Both Would Like to Thank . . .

We would like to especially thank Noreen Taylor, for her obedience to God's calling to pray for us and the Spiritually Unequal Marriage ministry, and for her generosity and willingness to read the first draft of our book.

We would also like to say thank you to all of our friends who share life with us at spirituallyunequalmarriage.com and our friends at 1Peter3Living. You bless us so much.

Finally, and most importantly, thank You, Lord Jesus. You are the reason we live and breathe.

Introduction

You are about to embark on an unexpected journey and we, the authors, Dineen and Lynn, will be traveling this unusual pathway with you. We are ordinary women and ordinary wives just like you. And, just like you, we believe that Jesus is the Son of God and our redeemer. Our husbands do not.

On your journey with us, you will experience the wonder of Scripture as it comes to life, filling you with truths that will rock your world and leave you with a fresh perspective and optimism. You will discover that Scripture is living and active and relevant to your marriage. We, Dineen and Lynn, believe that 2 Corinthians 6:14, "Do not be yoked together with unbelievers," is a firm calling by God to all unmarried believers. However, we also know that many of us arrive in a spiritually mismatched union and desire to honor God with our marriage. This book is for all of us who are traveling the path of the spiritually mismatched.

As we travel this route, you will discover that no matter how you arrived in your unequally yoked marriage, God's plans for your marriage and your future are fantastic and may take turns that are often unexpected. Our Lord is the master of redeeming our past and our pain to reveal a life He has always desired for us to live. Because of this, you will discover a hope so wild that you will thrive in your zany yet challenging marriage.

We know too well that the married life of the unequally yoked isn't an easy one, and we understand the struggle to be a person of faith within a mismatched marriage relationship. We have experienced the heartache of walking alone in our belief in Christ. And we understand the challenges of making a marriage work with a partner who doesn't share the same worldview.

But we also have found healing and wholeness along the way, and it's our greatest desire to share with you what the Lord can do in a unique marriage such as ours. And we don't want one more woman to waste another minute searching for the truth God has so generously shared with us.

Our passion was set in motion in 2006, when Lynn followed God's leading to start the online ministry Spiritually Unequal Marriage. During this time, God brought the same calling to Dineen's heart and led her to Lynn. We complete each other for this ministry, sharing practical wisdom and heart lessons with our readers, and ultimately to honor and glorify God.

Our online ministry's purpose is to bring hope, practical help, encouragement and healing through the Lord, Jesus Christ, to others who are spiritually mismatched. God put a burning in our heart to share the keys to living abundantly—to thriving—as we walk out our faith within marriage.

It's our delight to share with you the victories promised to all of us through Christ. From this ministry we offer this book to you, our sisters, who are walking with us in a spiritually mismatched marriage.

Each of the 10 chapters provides a key principle to thriving in your spiritually mismatched marriage. Near the end of each chapter, we have included discovery questions designed to help move you closer to Christ and discover practical steps to grow in your marriage. We know it won't be easy to look deeply into places that have lived in darkness for perhaps years, but the promise of freedom awaits. At the end of each chapter is a prayer of commitment to "seal the deal." Make these prayers your own and then watch what God does. You will not be disappointed. God is anxiously waiting to unleash His wild hope in you and your marriage.

At the back of the book are additional resources for you to use on your journey: a discussion about children in a mismatched marriage, specific Scriptures shared by our readers that can bring comfort and hope as you pray them for your spouse and for yourself, and ideas for creating a family faith record so that one day you can share what your spouse missed before he came to faith. We have also included a study guide that can be used in a small-group setting.

We pray you will discover in these pages not just the promise of hope, but also that you will experience healing, find encouragement and realize you are not alone. You *can* thrive in your marriage. Ultimately, we pray that your life and marriage will bring honor to the name of Jesus Christ.

It's our pleasure and joy to pray for you. You can always find us at our website, www.spirituallyunequalmarriage.com. Come visit us whenever you can. We'll be there.

With hearts filled with eternal love,
Lynn Donovan and Dineen Miller

Meet Lynn Donovan

Jesus continued: "There was a man who had two sons. The younger one said to his father, 'Father, give me my share of the estate.' So he divided his property between them. "Not long after that, the younger son got together all he had, set off for a distant country and there squandered his wealth in wild living. After he had spent everything, there was a severe famine in that whole country, and he began to be in need. So he went and hired himself out to a citizen of that country, who sent him to his fields to feed pigs. He longed to fill his stomach with the pods that the pigs were eating, but no one gave him anything. "When he came to his senses, he said, 'How many of my father's hired men have food to spare, and here I am starving to death! I will set out and go back to my father and say to him: Father, I have sinned against heaven and against you. I am no longer worthy to be called your son; make me like one of your hired men.' So he got up and went to his father. "But while he was still a long way off, his father saw him and was filled with compassion for him; he ran to his son, threw his arms around him and kissed him. "The son said to him, 'Father, I have sinned against heaven and against you. I am no longer worthy to be called your son.' "But the father said to his servants, 'Quick! Bring the best robe and put it on him. Put a ring on his finger and sandals on his feet. Bring the fattened calf and kill it. Let's have a feast and celebrate. For this son of mine was dead and is alive again; he was lost and is found.' So they began to celebrate.

LUKE 15:11-32, EMPHASIS ADDED

Hello, my name is Lynn Donovan, and I am a prodigal daughter.

I arrived in my unequally yoked marriage during a period of my life when I was far away from Jesus. I left the faith of my childhood to chase the promises of happiness the world said belonged to me. Convinced that I needed only to reach out and grab hold of those promises, I bought into the lies that career achievements, expensive clothes and great vacations were certain to bring me happiness.

As a child, I attended church with my family. I came to believe in Jesus and I knew that He was the Son of God. I understood that He loved me and that I could pray to Him. Somehow, I knew that He was around me. But as years marched by and as I grew into young adulthood, my belief faltered. I conveniently ignored the lessons I had learned in my Sunday School days.

As a confident young woman (translation: arrogant), I knew what was best for me, and I firmly seated myself on the throne of my life and stepped onto the path of the prodigal.

It was during this time that I met my husband. He was different from me. He had life experiences I found exciting. He lived in a big city; he was a smart, science-minded guy who was well educated; and his perspective about living was fascinating and vastly different from where I came from. I was intrigued. We fell in love.

We were married within a year. We settled into a typical married life: We lived for career, the weekends and ourselves. I married fully aware of my rebellion against God's wisdom. I knew better.

I remember it was about three years into our marriage when discontentment arrived and settled in my heart. I discovered that living the way of the world was proving shallow. I felt lost and desperately unhappy.

Thoughts of my faith and of Jesus wouldn't leave me. An unexpected yearning grew inside—a yearning for Jesus. He was in relentless pursuit of that little Sunday School girl, and finally my discontentment allowed me to hear His voice. I returned to the faith of my childhood. The prodigal daughter came running home to her Father.

I hurried home, hand in hand with Jesus; and as I went, I dragged along my new husband, who kicked and screamed from the beginning. To say he was miffed about this "new man" in my life is a serious understatement. After all, he didn't believe in this "God stuff."

I quickly realized that my husband and I were at odds about a great many things. We were living in a marriage where we each held a different worldview. Our core values did not match. We were unequally yoked.

Through the early years of our marriage, I had recognized and struggled through this unique spiritual mismatch. I felt lonely. If I mentioned my faith or the name Jesus around my husband it was like lighting a short fuse to a bomb. Within minutes tension would ramp up in our home, so I quickly learned that in order to keep the peace, I had to hide my faith. I just wouldn't talk about it. Not an easy task for a woman. An entire part of my life, which was growing in importance, became a secret from my life partner. My heart ached to tell my spouse about the changes taking place in me. But my husband wasn't interested. I was baffled about this turn in our relationship. I wondered how I could be married and yet feel so lonely.

I wanted us to attend church together, like other couples. He wouldn't go. Arguments over issues in the news or over local politics and even over how to raise our kids became frequent in our house. It seemed to me that we were taking opposing sides about everything. The pain we both felt from our mismatched life was real and, at times, almost unbearable. I hurt. He hurt. And the cycle went on and on.

Years of the hurt cycle began to take a toll. Would we make it? During this period, I knew clearly God's desire for marriage.

I desperately wanted to honor Him, but what little peace we still had at home, the one place where peace should breathe, was disintegrating. I needed some godly advice, and I was desperate to find another woman who knew what I was feeling.

I discovered a couple of books—*When He Doesn't Believe* by Nancy Kennedy and *Surviving a Spiritual Mismatch in Marriage* by Lee and Leslie Strobel—that helped me gain perspective. But I wanted more. I longed for support as I struggled with the loneliness of loving the Lord and loving my husband, who was an atheist.

Years passed and slowly over time, Jesus arrived in our marriage. First, He began to work in me. Then the power and supernatural love of Jesus Christ began to transform the relationship between my husband and myself. Finally, both my husband and I experienced a peace in our home that had eluded us for many years. I moved from being frustrated and angry with my spouse to feeling earnest love and respect for him. Today, we are thriving in our marriage in spite of our spiritual differences. I have learned the keys to living life to the fullest with my husband and with Jesus as my Lord.

The healing in my marriage is a gift from God. I found the way through the unique struggles of attending church alone, finding common ground with my spouse and maintaining love when our hearts are divided over moral and spiritual issues. I discovered the amazing reality that through Jesus, a woman can live happily in her unequally yoked marriage.

Today, my husband and I are head over heels in love. We laugh together, raise our daughter and son as one, live for the adventure of life, and are at peace with my faith. We still face disagreements from time to time, just like any other couple. Our marriage is far from perfect; but we are healed and happy.

The Lord has done so much in the heart of my husband. I continue to trust that God is moving him forward in his journey toward the cross. I pray every morning the words of Romans 10:10:

> For it is with your heart that you believe and are justi-
> fied, and it is with your mouth that you confess and
> are saved.

Throughout our marriage, I've had the profound privilege to enjoy a front-row seat as I watch the Lord pursue my husband's soul. And I fall on my knees in utter amazement as the Lord continues to set me on paths of new adventures and unimaginable dreams. I have been part of the story where God orchestrated a landscape contractor named Joe to play a part in praying with my husband in the yard. I giggled with glee when a Mylar balloon arrived out of the sky to gently rest against our back door. My husband brought it in and read to me what was written on it: "Baptized." He asked, "Do you think this is a hint?" We laughed until our sides hurt. Of course, it was a hint!

Each day is an adventure and a lesson in love. I look forward to every minute of what the Lord has for me, my husband, our children and the world around me.

I can confidently tell you that no matter what may happen with my husband and his faith, I am living in triumph. I am living the abundant life that Jesus promised in John 10:9-10:

> I am the gate; whoever enters through me will be saved.
> He will come in and go out, and find pasture. The thief
> comes only to steal and kill and destroy; I have come
> that they may have life, and have it to the full.

All of this abundance came about because I met Jesus Christ on this crazy, mixed-up journey of an unequally yoked marriage. My husband's unbelief was the catalyst to my deep and vibrant faith. For that, I can say I am truly thankful.

I am an ordinary, everyday kind of woman. If the Lord will work the extraordinary in my life, He will do the same for you. It is my fervent prayer that you will discover the healing and restoring power of Jesus Christ in your life and marriage. Thank you for joining me for the journey ahead through the pages of this book. I pray that your life will be forever changed and that the name of Jesus will be honored within your marriage.

Please write me and tell me what the Lord is doing in your life.

With eternal love,
Lynn Donovan

Meet Dineen Miller

And we know that in all things God works for the good of those who love him, who have been called according to his purpose.

ROMANS 8:28

One of my most vivid childhood memories was the feel of the water trickling over my head at my baptism. I was four. Although I couldn't read, I would sit in my bed at night with the small Bible I'd received that special day, loving the feel of the parchment and the sound it made as I turned each semi-translucent page. I think that was my first experience of God's holiness.

Although I didn't grow up in a Christian home, my mother was diligent about exposing me to church as a young child. God ingrained Romans 8:28 into me from an early age. I knew before I ever read this verse that He brought something good out of everything.

I basically wandered in and out of God's presence throughout my teenage years and young adulthood. During this time I met my husband, and like so many college students, I became enamored with my career and the future with him. We did life just like we thought we were supposed to—got married, had kids, built our dream house.

Everything seemed perfect, yet I found myself wishing I could hide under the covers instead of facing the world each day. I had everything I could imagine wanting in my life, but I still felt unexplainably empty and dissatisfied. I wanted some kind of purpose in my life. I *needed* purpose.

Then, just as I'd started down the path of going back to college for my second degree, God inserted Himself into my wandering path and grabbed my attention. He let me know that it was time to quit living for myself and start living for Him.

From that moment on, I was enamored with God and His Word. I remember carrying my Bible around constantly those first few weeks, because it was like reading the latest *New York Times* bestseller. I suddenly sprang out of bed in the mornings, instead of wanting to hide.

I found a church, dove into ministry, and pursued God like I never had before. Shortly thereafter, my husband bought a Bible. I figured that by just reading it, he would become as enraptured with it as I had been. He'd gone to church sporadically as a child and during college when he was searching for answers in his life. I thought surely he would soon join me in my walk with Christ.

Not so. The Bible wound up collecting dust, and my hope lagged. I would ask him to come to church, but he would always refuse. About a year into my faith journey, my husband finally confided to me that he'd decided he was an atheist. I was devastated. The thought hadn't even entered my mind that he would make such a decision. And though he'd chosen not to share my faith, he gave me the freedom to pursue my own.

But on Sundays, I would see other families and ache for my husband to come around. Many Sundays I wept, resentful of my husband's disassociation with my faith. To me, it was my life; to him, it was something I did, like a hobby. I felt alone and misunderstood, and I found it easier to keep my faith to myself than to face the conflicts it seemed to stir in our house. Thus began my journey as an unequally yoked spouse.

We moved to Europe several years later for my husband's work. I felt confident that this was where God wanted us, and I expected an adventure, which it was until our girls started school. Our oldest, nine at the time, was picked on, ostracized and even "mobbed." (What we Americans know as stalking, Europeans call mobbing. Since this time, school officials along with parents have actively addressed this growing problem.)

I railed at God, wondering why He would allow such a thing to happen. I prayed and prayed, but nothing changed. Life became more about survival from one day to the next.

During this time, God taught me His amazing faithfulness. He taught me how to wait, trust and believe. I also discovered a group specifically for the unequally yoked, and I realized for the first time that I was not alone. The group I joined met monthly to share the ache in our hearts. We focused on aligning our hearts with God and living the 1 Peter 3 model of witnessing to our husbands. Together, we studied *Beloved Unbeliever* by Jo Berry and *Spiritually Single* by Marcia Mitchell. Through these books and the precious women I grew to love dearly, God started to change my heart and move my perspective from me and what I wanted to what was truly at stake: my husband's eternal security.

That's when I learned to adore my precious husband and appreciate the man who'd taught me more about forgiveness than anyone besides Jesus. I began to realize how this man, even though he didn't share my faith, had helped me to grow in so many ways. And I learned that I needed to look to God for my deepest needs—not my husband, who was never intended to fill that role.

My husband and I found a sort of harmony in our marriage that embraced a respect for one another's choices in faith. Over the years, God has continually shown me how to love my husband unconditionally. So much of our past conflicts became the strength of our marriage when we faced a life-threatening crisis with one of our daughters. This strength was the source of our unity when she was diagnosed with a malignant brain tumor, and it continues to bring us closer as we support each other through her ongoing recovery.

God is teaching me that life is not a problem to be solved but a gift to be enjoyed. I used to think that one day our lives would be free of trials. Now I understand that these trials are vital to our faith deepening and for us to draw closer to a God who loves us more than we are able to comprehend. God lets us go through the tough stuff so that we can each grow closer to being a reflection of the image of Christ. This training allows each of us to be a vessel of revelation to those around us of God's amazing goodness, mercy and grace and a reflection of Jesus to our husbands.

Sometimes survival is all we can do, and God asks nothing more, but He never intends for us to stay in that place. He wants us to thrive in our lives and in our mismatched marriages. And, ever the gentleman, God leaves the choice to us.

So what do you choose, dear friend? Choose to thrive, because I am so excited to be on this journey with you. It is one of the greatest honors and privileges of my life. This is Romans 8:28 in full swing, the chance to see God bring good—healing and hope—from the sharing of what He's done in my life. And He'll do the same for you, because you are His beloved one and His desire is for you.

Get ready to thrive. God's waiting to show you the way through the pages of this book. I hope that one day you'll share your story with me and let me know how God brought you to experience His wild hope.

Praying and believing,
Dineen

KEY #1

Know that You're Not Alone!

(Lynn)

And surely I am with you always, to the very end of the age.
MATTHEW 28:20

I don't care anymore. I need to be here, even if he won't come with me.

I made a beeline to the nearest seat in the back of the church; I felt the eyes of those already seated watching my determined steps. *Did they notice I was alone?* I quickly flipped the bulletin open, pretending to give it my complete attention; it was the only cover available to disguise my uneasiness. My anxiety over my situation slid into restlessness. I shifted awkwardly in my seat. After a few minutes, I settled down and ventured a glance around me. No one was staring. *Whew!*

My lips tipped up in a shallow smile. *I did it. I finally made it to church.* Today was a big day. I had left my comfort zone, and for the first time since being married I had made it to church—and I had gone alone.

As I waited for the service to begin, my thoughts returned to the struggle earlier in the morning. I recalled absent-mindedly applying mascara. I was calm and collected on the outside, yet on the inside, a battle raged. I was desperate to attend church but completely stressed out over the thought of attending alone.

I stood before the mirror and fought to gain control of my growing anger. Sealing the cap of the mascara, I stepped back and glanced across the bedroom to the lump of snoring covers. I seriously toyed with the idea of throwing my hairbrush at said lump in hope that it would inflict bodily harm. However, I steadied my resolve and then walked out of the house, determined not to start a fight or miss church one more week, even if I had to sit abandoned.

For years, my husband had refused to go to church with me. In fact, any mention of church, religion or faith had inevitably resulted in an argument, coupled with pouting, crying and/or manipulation—I'd resorted to them all. I had pleaded with him to be part of this world of mine. But he was adamant: "I don't buy into all this 'God stuff.'"

Finally, the service began. A silent breath of relief escaped my lips as the praise team took the stage. *Perhaps no one will notice me sitting here all by myself.*

That's when it happened. A young couple scooted into the chairs in front of me; naturally, they were holding hands. My chest tightened as I watched the man lean toward his wife's face. He flashed her an I'm-so-in-love-with-you-and-glad-to-be-in-church-with-you smile. I caught my breath and immediately looked down at my folded hands resting in my lap. Emotion welled up from within and ran over me. This couple's innocent exchange ripped open a pain in my chest.

Suppressed longing swelled out of control and then began to cool into a growing and familiar resentment. All of a sudden, I didn't like this couple so much. They represented everything I was missing in my marriage. Of course, the unsuspecting twosome had no idea how much I desperately wanted what they took for granted. I yearned to sit with my husband in church. I dreamed of holding his hand or looking up a Bible verse together and smiling over the intimacy of a shared faith.

The service continued. I could hear singing around me, but I was only vaguely aware of it. Finally, I lifted my head as the pastor took his place for the message. I tried to focus, but it was useless. His words floated off over my head, unheard. My thoughts fixated on this happy couple and on what they had that I didn't.

My loneliness intensified.

The Alone Factor

For most believers, attending church is an uncomplicated, enjoyable experience. Yet for the spiritually mismatched, our time spent in church can be a giant point of contention and conflict with our husband and even within our self. And it's not just church. We, the unequally yoked, often feel alone in many aspects of our marriage.

So how is it that many of us who believe in Christ and the Word of God find ourselves in a place such as this, a spiritually mismatched marriage? How can we be married and yet alone? Our struggles are unique when compared to marriages where faith isn't an issue. But what do we do about the faith gap in our relationship with our spouse?

These are great questions. As we explore the truths of living, loving and thriving in a spiritually mismatched marriage, we will look to God's Word for our truth. We can depend on the Lord to show us where we are today in our marriage and where He wants us to be in the future. We have a few laughs ahead, some freedoms to discover, maybe a tear or two and a marriage to revive. Are you ready to find the hope you have been missing? Then let's get started.

Do not be yoked together with unbelievers. For what do righteousness and wickedness have in common? Or what fellowship can light have with darkness? (2 Cor. 6:14).

If you have picked up this book, it's likely that you are keenly aware of this verse. In fact, you are living smack in the middle of this passage every day. This verse can be a heavy load on your soul at times, yet it serves as a light to truth. So, how is it that women, even believing women, find themselves in an unequally yoked marriage?

There are actually several different paths. In the beginning of this book, I shared with you my story. If you remember, I stepped away from my faith and took the prodigal route. I don't pretend that I didn't know the biblical teachings of 2 Corinthians 6:14. I just flat out ignored God's command and married my unbelieving fiancé, thinking that I knew what was best for me. I was convinced that my man would see the light quickly after our wedding. Dineen found faith as a young girl, yet she also floundered for a period of time. She fully returned to her faith when her girls were little. I find that this is common for many women who married an unbeliever. Becoming a parent often stirs women to return to faith.

During the past several years, women who are distraught over the faith differences in their marriage have shared almost every conceivable story with me as to how they arrived in their mismatched marriage. One woman told me that her spouse outright lied, telling her before they married that he was a believer. Many more have shared with me that their husbands assured them they believed in Christ but after the wedding ceremony, they discovered that their husband's faith was insincere or was dead.

It matters not how we came to be in our crazy, mixed-up and unexpected marriage situation. What matters is that God desires that we honor our marriage commitment and fulfill our marriage vows through His power and His strength. We can't do it on our own. Trust me, I have tried.

I assure you that I haven't figured everything out about thriving in this unique marriage, but I have learned a few things over the many years of loving Jesus and loving my husband. My journey was difficult and there were many years of confusion, sadness and unfulfilled expectations. I shed many tears along the way. Yet the Lord redeemed every lost moment and hurt. He alone restored my marriage and my heart. I discovered that it is possible to love, live and thrive in an unequally yoked marriage. So today I will make a bold promise to you. If you earnestly put into practice the 10 principals we uncover in this book, God will honor your efforts as well.

God wastes nothing. I am proof of this statement. He took my arrogant decision to marry an unbeliever and worked through it to show me a great number of things about myself and even more about His love, sovereignty and generosity. He flipped my life and marriage upside down, turned me inside out and used everything for His glory and my good. Today, I am happy in my unequally yoked marriage. My husband and I enjoy a thriving, meaningful and love-filled relationship because of Jesus Christ, even as my husband remains a skeptic. If the Lord will do this in an ordinary gal's life such as mine, He will do it for you too.

Is It Really Possible to Thrive in a Mismatched Marriage?

At the beginning of the chapter, I shared my story of stepping out of my comfort zone and attending church alone. I wonder if you've experienced something similar in your own mismatched marriage. In the years of working in ministry with women who are walking this marriage road, I have found one common thread all of us face at some point: We are lonely.

It's a strange paradox, loneliness and marriage. We arrive at this desolate place in our relationship, baffled by our spouse's hostility toward our faith. We yearn for peace to return to our home, yet we are at a loss about how to restore it. We are bewildered, because our home should be *the* one safe place where we can be our authentic self. We had believed that we would never feel lonely and would always feel loved and accepted. Instead of safety and security, however, what we discovered was the reality of ongoing struggles that result from conflicting worldviews, opposing political preferences and clashing notions of morality.

These conflicts aren't minor irritants in the skin of our relationship. Our core beliefs are the ideals that make us who we are. In a spiritually mismatched marriage, these core beliefs are under constant pressure and scrutiny. Arguments over faith can be frequent, and they can wear us out and emotionally wound us. After several years of living with the conflict, we may conclude that it is safer to avoid talking about our faith—it's in our best interest to keep that part of our lives hidden. And the loneliness sets in and grows.

Isolation steals our happiness, and bitterness breeds. We love our spouse, yet navigating our unequally yoked life proves thorny. Eventually we wonder if it is possible to thrive in our marriage.

Well, today, I have a single word for you: yes.

Yes, you can thrive. It *is* possible to live out your beliefs, love your spouse and overcome the faith barriers in your marriage. What I discovered after years of frustration and confusion is the first key to thriving in an unequally yoked marriage: You are not alone.

Recognizing that Jesus is with you always and is intimately involved in your marriage is life changing. Listen to this promise recorded in the book of Hebrews. It became my lifeline.

God has said, "Never will I leave you; never will I forsake you" (Heb. 13:5).

After a considerable amount of time, it finally clicked in my blonde brain that my husband's unbelief wasn't the problem in our life—*I* was the problem. I had unwittingly yet firmly established myself as the supreme ruler on the throne of my heart. As a well-known television personality would ask, "How's that workin' for ya?" I can respond, "It isn't."

It was time to kick myself off the throne of my life and let Jesus take His rightful place. Someone in my marriage needed to change and it wasn't going to be my spouse (darn it!). Therefore, it was up to me. I took a brave step: I threw my self-centeredness off the throne of my life and firmly seated Christ there instead. When I did, Jesus began to move me from loneliness to authentic fulfillment.

I wasted years looking to my husband to fulfill my every longing. Finally, I realized it was impossible for him to measure up to the enormous expectations I'd assigned him. I wrongly believed that it was my mate's responsibility to satisfy my every dream, desire or wish. What I discovered instead was that Jesus was the only One capable of fulfilling my longings.

This was a lightbulb moment for me. Placing Christ on the throne of my life allowed me to release my spouse from my ridiculous self-proclaimed entitlements. I turned to Jesus and He filled me with love, confidence and validation, giving freely everything I needed and more. When this happened, my spiritual journey, which had been stuck in infancy for years, energized. My love relationship with Christ came alive. From that time on, I experienced surprising changes. My love for my spouse exploded. Forgiveness came easier. Arguments diminished. The need to win at all costs disappeared. All of the struggles gone, swept away.

Joy returned to our home. Peace pervaded our relationship and, most astounding, my marriage was revitalized. I stopped placing unrealistic pressure on my mate. I found freedom and so did my husband. He was free to seek the truth without my manipulation. Our relationship matured in intimacy, love and acceptance.

Placing Christ on the Throne

When we throw ourselves off the power seat and allow Jesus to fill our soul, heart and mind—our whole life—with His leadership, the troubling, painful and fearful circumstances of our life lose their power over us.

If we begin every day by placing Christ first in our lives, God is going to radically intervene. But how do we place Christ on the throne of our life? We will cover that in detail in chapter 2, but for now, I have a simple exercise that I want you to try that will help you get started. For the next 30 days, when you wake up, immediately step out of bed, fall to your knees and pray something like this:

> *Jesus, right now as I begin this new day, I surrender my place of authority over my life to You. I am placing You firmly on the throne of my life. Teach me to focus on Your desires for living. I give You my entire life this day. In Your powerful name, Jesus, amen.*

I think that the first time I fell out of bed to my knees, I felt a little strange. I wondered what my husband would think if he rolled over and saw me on the floor. I also was skeptical that a tiny prayer said straight out of bed could make a difference in my life. However, after about a week, this humbling practice brought me into a deeper relationship with the Lord. Placing Christ on the throne of my heart birthed a new perspective and a brand-new hope. I slowly started to believe that I could overcome the difficulties in my life, and Jesus could handle my unbelieving spouse.

Whispering this small prayer as I start my day gives me perspective as the events of the day unfold.

Jesus with "Skin On"

The changes in my relationship with God and my spouse emerged slowly, however, and for years I struggled with common issues we all face in a uniquely yoked marriage, such as:

- How can I be submissive to my husband when he is not a believer?
- I want to tithe, but he doesn't agree. What can I do?
- How can I raise my children to know Jesus if my husband objects?
- How do I handle media choices?

These are defining and dividing issues between a believing spouse and a non-believing spouse. I looked to the Bible for godly advice and I found great wisdom there. But I still felt as if I needed guidance to apply the Word to my everyday life. I looked to my church, but I quickly discovered that specific teaching for the spiritually mismatched is a rarity on Sunday morning. However, I didn't give up. I kept searching for others who actually knew what living with an unbeliever felt like.

I am convinced that in the early years of my marriage, I could have avoided the loneliness and many of our marital conflicts if someone had come alongside me with godly advice. I yearned for guidance, assurance and support to persist through the hills and valleys of marriage. I needed friends who understood my situation. I hungered for the wisdom of other like-minded believers.

You might be surprised to know that there are many spouses—men and women—who travel this strange road of mismatchdom. Comfort comes from knowing there are others out there. We only need to seek each other out and connect. Recognizing that we are not the only person living in an unequally yoked marriage is a key aspect to restoring hope. Finding others and learning from them how to overcome major obstacles in a uniquely yoked marriage is life changing.

I first found this sort of friendship in a few unexpected places. First, I found it through a women's Bible study. This environment provided a haven where I was free to discuss my faith and ask questions that I was unable to voice within my marriage. In this small group, I found strength and friendship. These women were Jesus with "skin on" to me. Connecting in a small-group setting with like-minded believers on a weekly basis renewed my spirit and refreshed my soul. I would return home with a smile and a kiss for my husband, filled with a fresh anointing of hope.

A few years later, I discovered a group of unequally yoked believers through the fantastic and strange world of the Internet. Through this online community, I found friends who were just like me, married to an unbeliever, dealing with the exact same challenges as I was. We shared (and continue to share) our struggles and our triumphs.

Among these fellow sojourners, I established understanding, friendship, prayer support, and love. These cyberbuddies became my extended family with whom I was safe to share my thoughts about God, marriage and my unbelieving spouse. This "online church" became my outlet for frustrations and a godly source of wisdom. Their highest priority was, and still is, to love and honor Jesus and their spouse. An online Christian group is indeed a strange lifeline. But God in His wisdom brought us together so that we might encourage each other toward living a life of abundance, specifically in our mismatched marriage. As the apostle Paul told the Thessalonians:

Encourage one another and build each other up, just as
in fact you are doing (1 Thess. 5:11).

My online family is a diverse crowd of married believers. Some
live with atheists; some with agnostics. There are those whose husbands practice different faiths such as Hinduism, Islam or Judaism.
There are spouses who only praise the god of football, golf and
some other weekend sport. There are those who are married to a
spouse who professes Christianity but doesn't walk the walk. Some
have recently joined the uneven journey, and others have traveled
the rugged road for more than three decades. Yet no matter how we
started our journey or how long we have traveled, we share a common bond: our faith in Jesus Christ. We need each other.

Today, I invite you to leave your loneliness behind and find a
community that understands you and will pray for you and love
you. God works through people. We need you, and you need us.
You can start by joining Dineen and me every day at our website,
www.spirituallyunequalmarriage.com. You can also find us at our
online discussion group, http://groups. yahoo.com/group/1Peter
3Living. Founded in 2006, this group's sole purpose is to encourage and support those who are committed to live out God's com-
mands found in 1 Peter 3:

> Wives, in the same way be submissive to your husbands so
> that, if any of them do not believe the word, they may be
> won over without words by the behavior of their wives. . . .
> Husbands, in the same way be considerate as you live with
> your wives, and treat them with respect as the weaker part-
> ner and as heirs with you of the gracious gift of life, so that
> nothing will hinder your prayers (1 Pet. 3:1,7).

In addition, don't forget to look to your local church for a
small Bible study group for a "skin on" community of people.

I never thought I would describe my spiritually mismatched marriage as *thriving*. But because of my vibrant relationship with Christ, my Bible study and my "skin on" buddies, I am able to say that I am at peace and thriving in my marriage, and so is my spouse. I am also able to wholeheartedly trust the Lord for my husband's salvation.

Having Christ in my life enables me to view my husband as the wonderful man God created, regardless of our differing beliefs. Christ lavishes His love on me, so I can pour it into my spouse. Now when Sunday morning arrives, I walk into church and head for the front row. I am unaware if people notice that I'm physically alone. Jesus lives in me. Why should I feel lonely? In the front pew, I sing with gusto, offering praise to God for a marriage overflowing with love and contentment and authentic joy. I praise the Lord as the King of my heart.

Discovery

Take a moment and ask God to meet you here through these questions, to bring freedom, resolution and encouragement to you. It's your day to receive wild hope.

1. What was one particular season of loneliness in your mismatched marriage?

2. Looking at the lessons in this chapter, what specific points can help to move you from loneliness to fulfillment?

3. Begin the morning prayer practice discussed in this chapter. How will you remind yourself to fall from the bed to the floor? Write out the short prayer you will pray.

4. How do reading God's Word and praying affect your marriage?

5. What does God's Word say concerning an unbelieving spouse? (See 1 Corinthians 7:12-15.)

6. What three issues in your marriage will you commit to pray for daily?

Prayer

Lord, thank You that I am never alone. You promised You would never leave me nor forsake me, and I will rest in this truth. Today I am committed to restoring happiness and hope to my marriage. Teach me to take my eyes off my circumstances and focus completely on You. I seat You firmly on the throne of my life.

Father, today I recommit my life and my marriage to You. Create a powerful yearning in me to meet with You every day. Teach me Your truths to live by and reveal Your desire for my life and the life of my spouse. Restore optimism in my heart for our future. Empower me to cling to my faith when my husband is unfriendly toward You.

Bring into my life other believers who are Jesus with "skin on." Lord, lavish Your love on me that I may pour it into my spouse, my family and a world desperate for a Savior. In Jesus' name I pray, amen.

Don't Save Your Husband—Save Yourself

(Lynn)

*Jesus answered, "I am the way and the truth and the life.
No one comes to the Father except through me."*

JOHN 14:6

There is a rumor floating around our house that some crazed, five-foot-four-inch blonde woman is a *control freak*. Ahem, well, I begrudgingly admit that it's true. It's my nature to want to oversee just about everything in my home. And over the years I have become pretty good at controlling many things. I have also become frustrated beyond reason over the things I can't control, such as my husband's salvation. Can you relate?

Why is it that we women possess this innate desire for control? We want jurisdiction over every detail of our life and the lives of our kids, our pets, our husband and even our neighbors. We like it when the universe spins around our idea of what is right.

I remember when my control-freak self hit a high point of activity about 10 years into our marriage. I was growing as a believer, but my husband remained in the same place he had been on the day we had married, an atheist. At the time, I faithfully read my Bible and prayed every single day, "Lord, save my husband." However, God wasn't answering me. I became confused and wondered why I was receiving the silent treatment.

Confusion turned to frustration; after all, the Bible told me that the salvation of my husband is God's perfect will. I can, however, admit today that what I had been praying was a selfish prayer. I had imagined that my man's salvation would make my life a great deal easier. Once saved, I reasoned, we would finally sit together in church as a couple. I had dreamed that he would encourage me to give our money to the ministries I loved. Once he came to faith, I was certain that he would insist on hosting a weeknight home group at our house. I just knew that if my husband would only become *saved*, we would live in marital bliss forever. I had lofty expectations; therefore, my self-proclaimed *calling* became bringing to the cross this lost soul whom I had married.

I went to work immediately. I diligently wrote Scripture verses on small index cards and strategically placed them around the house. My best work was the bright pink card taped to the bathroom mirror. I was convinced the Scripture verse on this card would compel my man to fall to his knees, moved by the truth. Then he would see the light. I envisioned him asking Christ into his life right there on the bathroom floor in his pj's.

It didn't work. After a month had passed, I realized that he wasn't reading them. In fact, I became conscious of his irritation when I discovered the pink card crumpled in the trashcan. My disappointment turned to annoyance. But I remained resolute to see my self-appointed mission through to the end.

Thus, the battle of two strong-willed people commenced. It wasn't pretty. Over the years, I became a specialist in spiritual ambush. My poor guy. Our poor marriage.

I know this kind of coercion can be common in an unequally yoked home. That's because we are desperate for our spouse to come to faith. When that doesn't happen right away, we decide to take matters into our own hands and we do some really stupid things that never work.

One day not long ago, I was curious what other wives tried in order to win their husbands to Christ. So I asked my blogging friends this question: "Can you please share with us some of the crazy, zany, stupid, waste-of-time efforts you undertook to save your husband?" Here are just a few of the responses we received:

Tina: The main thing I can remember doing is leaving my Bible out and open or leaving one of my Bible studies nearby, so he could see it. Unfortunately, he's not as nosy as me and never even paid any attention to what I was doing!

Tish: I signed up at church to read the Bible through in a year and decided I would do it aloud in bed with my husband listening to every word. Boy, did that go over like a load of bricks.

Stacy: I never did anything crazy . . . probably he would see them as annoying . . . leaving the Bible or devotionals open to certain pages . . . articles left lying in strategic places . . . and . . . the Post-it notes. Don'cha just love how those come in so many colors? I always try to pick the colors that stand out. :) I do admit to using the Post-its still . . . but it's more for me now. But, of course, anyone else is welcome to read it.

Tamara: I did a lot of zany things: (1) Left brochures on his night table and then I got angry when he put his auto magazines on top of the brochures without reading them. (2) Invited my Christian friends over to try to convert him. (3) Played my worship songs until he left the room. (4) Here is something I still do and what I really need to stop—My husband will ask me a simple question about faith and I get on my soapbox and have a sermon. He usually turns away after a few minutes and complains, "Honey, I only wanted an answer, not a sermon." Then I am insulted that he isn't more impressed with my "wise" words.

I laugh out loud when I read some of these. I guess it gives me comfort to know I am not alone. The point I want to make here is this: Our hearts are in the right place. We deeply desire an honest and full salvation experience for our unbelieving spouse. However, our controlling nature can often get in the way of that experience; and in fact, our manipulations in the name of Christ often backfire.

Unbelieving husbands find themselves in a strange place when it comes to our faith. Many men feel threatened by this "new man" in our life. They can't see Him, let alone compete. Read what one wife, Angela, shared about her husband:

When I returned to the Lord, I was on fire and even wrote an email to all my friends and family about my new discovery of God's forgiveness and grace. My husband and I had been married for about three years and I had just graduated from college. We didn't have kids yet. I was involved with a local church and attended every time I could. My husband would make comments to make it clear he was feeling neglected and wanted me to spend time with him. I pretty much let him know that if he wanted to spend time with me, he would need to go to church with me. That did not go over too well at all. In the end, it just made him feel like he had to compete with God for my affection. One day he even told me this—He said it was not fair because if it were any other guy, he could just show up at his house, punch him and tell him to stay away. But in this case he couldn't compete. He seemed so rejected and defeated when he told me this that it was like a punch in the gut for me. That is when I realized I was handling the entire situation wrong. (Of course, that did not stop me from doing other little stupid things along the way!) Now I've learned the best thing to do is love him unconditionally and pray for him. But it has taken me quite a few years, tears and silly crazy mistakes to get to this point.

Angela's words ring with truth, and I can tell you after years of working with unequally yoked women that many of our men feel this way. And, to top it off, we wives feel exactly like Angela. At some point, we've discovered that we've wasted too much time and endured unnecessary heartache.

I made multiple blunders while stuck in my ambush way of thinking. My husband and I were both miserable due to the constant pressures and conflict, which I had created. Of course, all my efforts to save my husband were fruitless. Duh! Then several years ago, I heard Christ speak to my heart. He clearly reminded me that my husband's salvation would be for His glory and not my own. Whoa, I needed that reality check. That is the day I quit placing religious tracts on my husband's pillow. I refrained from engaging him in conversations that would force a discussion of faith. Those feeble attempts were actually pushing my husband further away from finding Christ.

It's Safe to Relinquish Control

In the Garden of Eden, after Adam and Eve had eaten from the Tree of the Knowledge of Good and Evil, the Lord appeared to them and stated that there would be a curse put on them because of their sin. Look at this passage in Genesis:

> You will desire to control your husband, but he will rule over you (Gen. 3:16, *NLT*).

So, this control game started with the very first couple. You and I have a desire within us to control, and this Scripture specifically points out our desire to control our husband. However, the verse goes on to say that the husband will rule over the wife. So where in this do we find a livable balance? That's a great question. I'm not sure I have it all figured out yet, but I have walked with the Lord and my unbelieving spouse for many years and have discovered that we can surrender our deep need for control.

How?

The key is to stop trying to save your husband and save yourself. Letting go might appear to be a scary proposition. You might be frightened to even think about releasing your husband, because you are the only believer he may encounter on a regular basis. You are likely the one person who is actively praying for him. And if you don't show him Jesus, who will? All of this is true, yet you are underestimating the power of the Lord in your life.

When I finally let go and stopped all my foolish and unproductive efforts to save my man, two things happened. First, I discovered new freedom. A terrible heaviness I didn't know I had been carrying lifted from my shoulders. I no longer felt the pressure to do whatever it takes to push my husband to faith. I stopped obsessing over what "activity" I should try next to force my husband toward faith. I was able to step back and finally trust God wholeheartedly with my husband's salvation. What a relief.

Second, my husband also experienced freedom. He no longer needed to deflect my ridiculous efforts. He finally relaxed. My faith in Jesus became much less of a threat in his eyes. In a strange turn of events, he suddenly grew curious about faith, even to the point where he purchased his own Bible. He was free to discover faith at his own pace, in his own way.

For years, I had tried to be Jesus. The best thing I ever did was to get out of the way so that Jesus could be Jesus. The truth of God's promises swallowed up my insecurity. I relinquished control and turned my man completely over to Christ. And you know what happened? An unexpected, peaceful freedom emerged in our marriage. Bickering over politics lessened. I no longer needed to always be right or to win every argument in defense of Christ. These are a few of the subtle but much-needed changes that revitalized our love.

Throw Me a Life Preserver!

Trusting Christ with our husband's salvation is only one step in the journey of the spiritually mismatched. We must leave our silly and unsuccessful attempts to convert our man behind us. However, as wives, we remain vitally important to our husband's faith journey. I have much to share with you about our fundamental role in their salvation later in the chapter but before we get there, I have a question: How do you save yourself?

There is one answer: Jesus.

You need a vibrant and deep relationship with the Redeemer. When you love Jesus inside and out, backward and forward, morning, noon and night, you will experience a powerful kind of love. A life wrapped in the love of Jesus discovers it's impossible to remain defeated in daily circumstances. It's also near impossible for your family to resist. The apparent love of Christ in your life will seep out of your heart and pour into your everyday activities. Your spouse and kids will feel it; they will notice and they will respond.

Like any relationship, cultivating friendship, intimacy and love requires time. It's the same with our Lord. We need to spend time in His presence. I discovered the life preserver I needed to save me from myself: time alone with God.

It was during the years of marriage struggles that my mother gave me a Daily Bible. I picked it up one morning, sat down and began reading. I didn't realize it at the time, but that very day I took a giant step into a love relationship that would forever change my life.

Every morning since, I rise early, before the rest of the house wakes. I shuffle into the kitchen, grab a steaming cup of strong coffee and head to the family room couch. There I spend the most important time of my day. I open my Bible and read God's Word. In the pages of this book, I meet with Jesus. Every morning. And He never fails to overwhelm me with love, compassion, forgiveness and self-control—absolutely everything I need and more to face the day. He fills me up so that I can pour out love on others, and He prepares me to tackle any challenges I may face.

God's Word is the blueprint for living a life filled with joy, fulfillment and purpose. That is the truth of this Scripture in Hebrews:

> For the word of God is living and active. Sharper than any double-edged sword, it penetrates even to dividing soul and spirit, joints and marrow; it judges the thoughts and attitudes of the heart (Heb. 4:12).

God's Word is living and active, and I will talk about it to anyone who will listen. The Word of God changed me and when I changed, my marriage was transformed in spite of the fact my husband remained a staunch unbeliever.

As I continue to read the Bible, I pray through the verses, asking God to make them real and to show me how to live them out in my ordinary life. For example, just this morning I was reading a passage in Matthew:

> Then Peter came to Jesus and asked, "Lord, how many times shall I forgive my brother when he sins against me? Up to seven times?" Jesus answered, "I tell you, not seven times, but seventy-seven times" (Matt. 18:21-22).

Forgiveness is an area in everyone that always needs reminding and refining. This is especially true for those of us in an unequally yoked marriage. I remember a time when my anger at my husband reached an all-time high in the early years of our marriage. Our spiritual disconnect left me feeling hurt and alone. I was disappointed with my situation and mad at my husband.

It was during this time that I remember sitting down for breakfast with one of my friends from my Bible study group. She listened patiently as I spewed my feelings. Then she suggested we study and pray together for our husbands. I looked across the table in astonishment and thought to myself, *Didn't she just hear a word I said?* I wouldn't even consider doing a Bible study that might benefit this man who was the source of my unhappiness. I was filled with that much anger. In reality, I *needed* a study exactly like what my friend had suggested, coupled with a large dose of forgiveness.

Forgiveness isn't easy, and I will share more about it in chapter 8. For now, though, as I think back on that selfish time in my marriage, I see how reading God's Word slowly and purposefully softened my attitude to the point where I could forgive and love with my whole heart.

The passage I read this morning filled me fresh with forgiveness. It also reminded me of the profound forgiveness granted to me through the resurrection of Christ. God's Word *is* living.

It *is* powerful. It *can* change a heart and a marriage, and it *can* bring freedom. I know this is true because God's Word changed little ol' me.

A Daily Prayer Life

Coupled with reading the Word of God, I began to pray. I struggled with purposeful prayers and distractions in the early years. Perhaps you are like me, easily distracted. I spy the dirty dishes waiting in the sink; or the dog paws at my leg and whines, wagging his tail, hoping I will get up to feed him. There are a thousand and one things vying for my attention.

However, I found a solution to my mind wandering: a simple and inexpensive journal. Writing out sentences in long hand brings my eyes and thoughts down to a single page. I leave the distractions of the room and focus on the paper and the words I am forming. I think clearly about the words I am offering in prayer. After writing a page or two, I find myself leaving the journal and speaking words.

Another benefit of prayer journaling is revisiting some of my old prayers. My soul swells when I see the faithfulness of God in how He answered my prayers, large and small, with His ingenious wisdom and great care. When the Lord doesn't answer a prayer the way I anticipated, I am often amazed to realize He had something different in mind, and His ways are always the best ways.

Sitting down with purpose and a prayer journal is just the beginning. What we pray, however, is what matters the most.

How Should We Pray?

Every morning I hold my husband in prayer, asking our great God for his salvation. I pray for his protection from the enemy. I ask the Lord to send godly men into his life. I cover his life with words spoken over every aspect of his career, health, parenting—every detail.

The specifics change through the years and seasons of marriage. For example, in the early years of our marriage, I would pray that the Lord would save my husband, give him a yearning to read the Bible, and open his spiritual eyes. These prayers are not wrong, but today I am moved to pray like this:

> *Oh, Father, today let me just love him. Pour Your love into*
> *me in such a powerful and complete way that I am just*
> *bursting with You. Teach me how to pour Your love out over*
> *my husband and everyone I meet. Make every encounter I*
> *have an opportunity for others to see You and not me.*
>
> *Father, I beg You to place Yourself before my man today.*
> *Be in front of him at the office. Be at his side at lunchtime.*
> *Be behind him as he talks on the phone and writes a letter.*
> *Lord, place Christian men in his path, at the store today, on*
> *the phone and at the office. Let him see reminders that You*
> *are in relentless pursuit of him and that Your passion for him*
> *will never fade. Lord, I ask You to surround him with You.*
> *Fill his morning, noon and night with Your presence*
> *and protect him from the enemy.*
>
> *Lord, I ask Your will in his life, not my will. I love You, Jesus.*
> *I love You. Your humble servant, Lynn.*

Toss out the index cards. They are a waste of time. The love of God in a woman who is fully committed to Christ is irresistible. You won't need to say a word to your man. Your loving actions will speak volumes (see 1 Pet. 3:1).

Loving the Lord is born out of time spent with Him. Reading His blueprint for life and praying are seemingly simple and as old as the ages. Yet time alone with God is rarely a priority in the life of a busy wife. I know—I was once that way myself. However, I made a commitment and a sacrifice to rise early, so I could spend time with God.

God has faithfully honored that sacrifice. He meets me every morning and I am never disappointed. He fills me with His wisdom, a fresh perspective, and peace. I close my Bible and prayer journal, feeling confident and fortified, able to face whatever the day brings—even a husband who is hostile to Jesus. I live with hope and I know happiness because, without a doubt, God holds my tiny life in the very palm of His hand.

This is our vital role in our husband's salvation: to love the Lord God with all of our heart, soul, mind and strength. Nothing more, nothing less.

The principles of this book center on this truth: Reading God's Word and praying can and will change a wife, a husband, a home, a marriage, a neighborhood and a world in desperate need of a Savior. That's a promise.

Prayer and daily Bible reading led me to peace. I am no longer distraught over our spiritual differences. Released is my desire to persuade, argue and manipulate my husband to faith. Jesus is completely capable of saving my doubter without my help, thank you very much.

I challenge you today to begin this love journey with Jesus. Make a daily appointment with the King and keep it. Duty will turn to desire, and you will never be the same. Like me, you will discover the abundant life.

Discovery

Please pray first that God would open your eyes and heart to meet Him here in these questions, to bring freedom, resolution and encouragement to you.

1. What was a time that you engaged in "spiritual ambush"?

2. How did your spouse receive your intervention? How did he feel about your efforts? How did that make you feel?

3. Look up 1 Corinthians 2:14. How does your understanding of this verse influence your prayer life? How does it affect your interactions with your spouse?

4. Most women enjoy talking—a lot. If you have this gift, how does 1 Peter 3:1 challenge you?

5. With regard to saving your spouse, are there specific actions you need to discontinue?

6. How do you see yourself reflecting Jesus to your family today?

Prayer

Lord Jesus, forgive me if I have been a stumbling block in my spouse's salvation experience. I turn over my will to Your capable hands and I will trust You to save my spouse in Your time and in a way that brings You honor.

Pour a fresh anointing of the Holy Spirit into me each morning to empower me to live my faith authentically before my spouse. Reveal to me the truth of 1 Peter 3:1 and how my words can bring healing or how they can hinder. Let me learn to love my husband with Your love. Let him find Your love irresistible.

Remind me daily that You are relentlessly pursuing my spouse and will never give up.

Teach me to pray effectively for my spouse, asking for salvation and protection from evil. I ask in the life-changing name of Jesus, amen.

KEY #3

Stay Connected
(Lynn)

Love is patient, love is kind. It does not envy, it does not boast,
it is not proud. It is not rude, it is not self-seeking, it is not easily
angered, it keeps no record of wrongs. Love does not delight in evil
but rejoices with the truth. It always protects, always trusts,
always hopes, always perseveres.

1 CORINTHIANS 13:4-7

The Pink Princesses. Who would have thought the Pink Princesses could profoundly affect the love between two people. Certainly not me. Who are the Pink Princesses, you ask? Well, they aren't a newly discovered Christian girl band. Nor a romantic comedy film that ends with my favorite five words: "They lived happily ever after." And the Princesses aren't characters from a romance novel.

The Pink Princesses is the name of my Fantasy Football team. Some of you are rolling your eyes about now, but stay with me because there are some amazing truths we can learn from this seemingly silly game.

I shared with you in chapter 1 that I felt lonely in the early years of marriage. My husband and I were suffering from a major disconnect. He didn't view life from my perspective, and I refused to consider his position. Our detachment from each other stemmed from the soul, deep in the heart. It then spilled over into our everyday living. We lost the simple joys of married life.

I distanced myself from him because I feared the pain caused by some off-hand comment from my spouse about Jesus. My husband distanced himself from me because he grew tired of the sharp word exchanges over issues he had firmly settled in his mind. We each withdrew behind skillfully crafted walls of protection.

This was a scary time in our marriage, as it can be for any marriage. It's precisely during this type of cool period that we must run—not walk—to the source of unconditional love and forgiveness. Our daily appointment with the King becomes crucial to navigate this season. Remaining connected to our spouse is also imperative. As a believing wife, God is calling us to be intentional, working to keep communication open and to love our spouse with purpose and without conditions. But how do we go about cultivating common interests and encourage love in a way that doesn't threaten our spouse and at the same time allows us to live authentically? This is a great question, and the Pink Princesses became my answer.

Many years ago, I read the book *His Needs, Her Needs* by Willard F. Harley, Jr. When I was a young wife, this book was instrumental in my understanding the needs of husbands and wives. Upon reading this book, it dawned on me that God made men and women vastly different—on purpose!

Now, after years of walking with God and my unbelieving spouse, I truly understand God's wisdom. The Lord used and continues to use my husband to wear down the sharp edges of my personality and craft the much-needed changes in my character. He often used my misunderstanding of the male psyche to file off a bad attitude and polish away selfish pride.

In Dr. Harley's book, I discovered that one of the five primary needs of a husband is to share recreational companionship. This ranks right behind sexual fulfillment, which we will touch on later in the chapter. A husband wants to have fun and wants to share fun with his best friend, his wife. This is our opportunity to pour our love into our marriage and participate in our husband's life in a nonthreatening way. For me, this turned out to be Fantasy Football.

My husband isn't an athletic person; however, he does enjoy watching a good football game on the weekend, and on occasion I would join him to watch a Denver Broncos game. But, like many women, my interest tended to wander off and focus on something other than uncivilized men running around in tights inflicting injury upon one another.

However, several years ago, my husband joined a neighborhood Fantasy Football League. During the course of the football season, I watched him morph into a crazed fanatic. He would intensely track the games, glued to the television and his laptop, checking stats and scores.

Some of us have strong feelings about football and sports in general. From September until the Super Bowl, football widows abound. Similarly, I remained outside of this large part of my husband's life. I would find myself drifting off to the computer or the kitchen. Most Sundays we spent together at home, yet we were still alone.

Then, as it happened, a spot opened up in my husband's Fantasy Football League. One day, he casually mentioned the opening to me.

"Why can't I join?" I asked.

"You want to play Fantasy Football?" he asked astonished.

"Yes, yes, I think I do," I grinned.

Actually, I jumped at the chance. I was determined to participate in this part of his world.

Did I know much about football? No. Did I know how to play Fantasy Football? I hadn't a clue, but I joined anyway.

Thus the Pink Princesses were born. My daughter named the team and selected our logo, a unicorn framed by a rainbow, a true girly team. This was my opportunity to connect with my husband, and I took it.

I made myself learn the game and the strategies. Interestingly, even our son and daughter became involved. They were quite surprised to see Mom and Dad watching football all day and having a blast. My husband and I spent the day on the couch together as a couple. Week after week, we talked over strategies and our players. We teased each other about our team's performance. We laughed, cheered, jeered and cajoled—and we loved.

We loved.

Love Is for a Lifetime

Let's read part of 1 Corinthians 13 again. This verse has been used so often by so many people that it has almost become a cliché, thereby losing some of its power in our lives. However, the truths it contains are there, and they apply to every marriage, including a spiritually mismatched one.

> Love is patient, love is kind. It does not envy, it does not boast, it is not proud. It is not rude, it is not self-seeking, it is not easily angered, it keeps no record of wrongs. Love does not delight in evil but rejoices with the truth. It always protects, always trusts, always hopes, always perseveres (1 Cor. 13:4-7).

Within these few sentences, God is freely giving us the secret to a long and joyful marriage. The precepts are specific and doable. Their simplicity is often underrated. Let's take a look.

"Love is patient, love is kind." Growing our patience is one of God's favorite things to do. Like me, you may have already discovered how often the Lord will use our husband to grow us up. Learning patience is a slow process and takes years of practice to perfect. Patience and kindness are really all about accepting our mate for who he is. It is letting go of our anger and frustration to simply love the man. This truth involves surrendering our long-held expectations and entitlements that we grip with a tight fist, believing they are rightfully ours. God's Word is clear about marriage. It doesn't say we are entitled to a home with two children, one cat and three dogs, a car, etc.

What we are entitled to is death, yet we received the gift of God's love and salvation through Jesus. This gift comes with fantastic promises as well as responsibilities. We as believers are commissioned to be servants to others. Serving is kindness in action. When we set this truth firmly in our hearts, the pain of unrealized expectations diminishes. Christ fills us with new dreams and expectations, which, in my experience, have proven to be extraordinary and wonderful.

"[Love] does not envy." The grass isn't greener on the other side of the hill. Being in love with our husband is a choice. In this passage, the Lord reminds us that we don't always feel the emotion of love. Although we might at times feel as if we are not in love with our spouse, each day we need to make the choice to remain in the marriage and pursue happiness through the transforming power of Jesus in our lives.

"[Love] does not boast, it is not proud. It is not rude, it is not self-seeking, it is not easily angered." These characteristics describe practical aspects of being considerate of our mate—truly one of those rubber-meets-the-road instances in marriage.

More than anything, men want respect. It is at the core of their being, and it's of paramount importance that they receive respect from their wife. Respect is vital for a marriage relationship to thrive. It can be challenging to respect some-one whom you know so much about—the good, the bad and the ugly. Yet the Lord is very specific to wives with regard to this need in men:

> However, each one of you also must love his wife as he loves himself, *and the wife must respect her husband* (Eph. 5:33, emphasis added).

I discovered an easy way to help turn myself away from crit-icism and toward respect. During my prayer time, I would write down the qualities I appreciated about my husband. My list would look something like this (these are only a few of the traits I admire in my husband):

> He is kind.
> He is a great dad.
> He is a hard worker and provider.
> He laughs at my silliness.
> He does the laundry.
> He is loyal.

I would bring these attributes before the Lord and thank Him for placing them in my husband. Guess what happened? Naming my husband's strengths and thanking God for each one opened my eyes to see the amazing person he really is. This seemingly elementary list removed my focus from the negative to see my spouse through the eyes of Christ. And you know what? He's one fantastic man.

"[Love] keeps no record of wrongs. Love does not delight in evil but rejoices with the truth." When I am wronged, I turn to the Lord, and I choose to forgive. Forgiveness is the glue in all marriages. Forgiveness isn't always easy and often takes time, but it's pos-

sible to forgive much because Christ forgave us. The truth is that something amazing happens when we forgive our spouse. We become free. This is a priceless place to live, and it is central to a thriving marriage.

"[Love] always protects, always trusts, always hopes, always perseveres." These traits are pretty easy to forget. I remember sitting among a group of women at a birthday party one night. The discussion turned to husbands, as it often does when a group of married women get together. Every woman there jumped on her husband with words that belittled and shamed their spouse. I am not innocent of this—I know I have shared in the gripe sessions in the past. However, this particular evening I became increasingly uncomfortable as I sat and listened. Ephesians 5:33 would not leave my mind. I remember the instructor at my weekly Bible study specifically speaking to this very moment. She said, "Respecting your husband means you never say something that would dishonor him." It was at that precise moment that I decided my husband-bashing days were over. My man deserved my loyalty, and nothing less.

Real love is steadfast, it's optimistic, it overlooks a multitude of shortcomings, and it never fails. Sounds like Jesus to me.

For me, joining the Fantasy Football League was living 1 Corinthians 13 out in real life. It's my deepest desire to love people as Jesus loved, to model the characteristics of this passage to my unbelieving husband. That kind of love is powerful and life changing, and over time it becomes irresistible.

Connecting with my husband requires a sacrifice of my time and perhaps some of my own desires; however, our marriage is richer for it.

At the end of the football season, the Pink Princesses played my husband's fantasy team for the Super Bowl in our league. It was a close game, and we enjoyed every single minute together. The Pink Princesses won the league title, beating my husband's team and my neighbors' teams as well. The old-timers who have played in the league for years and who are still waiting for their first league title are probably miffed that a harebrained, five-foot-four-inch blonde girl, who named her team with a girly name, won the whole thing. Oh, the irony. What was most important about the experience, though, was that my husband and I had a blast throughout the season, and we can't wait to do it again next year.

So make a plan to connect with your husband. Be intentional. Dineen started playing Disc Golf with her husband last year. But your plan doesn't need to include sports. Noreen enjoys taking long walks with her husband. Perhaps it is just sitting together while he is working in the garage, or joining him on a bike ride. Think about what *he* enjoys, and join in. Make every effort to connect with your unbelieving spouse. Remember, you have the power of the Holy Spirit in you. Allow the Lord to love your husband through you. When you start giving 100 percent, most men respond and give back.

I will add here that I made the decision to miss church on some Sundays so I could spend time with my husband. I recognize that the "church or no church" question is a contentious issue in a spiritually mismatched marriage. But it is appropriate to love our husbands with our time, and that time can include Sunday mornings.

Remember, our relationship with the Lord is built during our daily quiet time. Church is a time of corporate worship and an opportunity to connect with other like-minded believers. Spending time in the house of the Lord is a privilege and believers need that weekly recharge. However, occasionally skipping services in order to spend time with our man is okay. Find a balance. For me, I want to be in church every Sunday. It feeds my soul. But I do give myself permission to miss a week here and there to spend time with my spouse.

All Things Are Not Equal

You might be wondering why it seems to always be up to you to change, to give, to love. What about him? Doesn't he have to do anything?

Our calling in marriage isn't to an equal partnership—although the world would have you believe it is. A successful and happy marriage requires a willingness to give all of ourselves. It's never a fair arrangement, and there will be days when we're convinced our efforts are worthless, especially when our own needs remain unmet.

The 1 Corinthians 13 passage is a tall order for a wife and can feel overwhelming when she is charged with loving a man who doesn't subscribe to biblical standards of love. Yet 1 Corinthians 13 calls into sharp focus the essence of unconditional love. It shouts to us as believers to love our husband with a commitment that is total and selfless. In truth, God is asking us to live out our love in the most difficult of circumstances, because it will accomplish His good and perfect will.

However, we can't do it by our own strength. Thankfully, the Lord stands ready to pour into us every perfect gift we need in order to walk this path of the uniquely yoked. He knows we can't do it alone, so we must run to the source and let Him fill us.

The marriage relationship is the greatest human display of God's love. And many people are watching us: our spouse, our kids, our friends, indeed an entire world desperate to discover a woman who loves with such intensity that it's courageous. In her, they see Jesus.

"We love because he first loved us" (1 John 4:19). Remember Jesus loved us first. He is teaching us to do the same, beginning with our husbands. I am convinced this is the way of the Lord.

Bring on the Bedroom

Creating connections with our spouse will carry forward to the bedroom. However, it's behind the bedroom door that marriages sure can struggle. It's no wonder, either, when you look at the trash coming from most media sources. Add to this the tension of our differing spiritual views, and some specific challenges arise.

Sex is a vital part of every great marriage. But in my years of working in ministry with women, I have discovered that a discussion about this subject is usually difficult and often carries with it a multitude of emotions. I often hear the following:

> I became a Christian about three years after I married my husband. He is hostile about my faith. He says this Jesus guy has taken his spot in our marriage. He also wants to do things in the bedroom that now make me uncomfortable. What do I do?

> My wife became a Jesus freak recently. It's only a matter of time before she becomes a prude in the bedroom. I am angry.

With such emotions running wild, how do we navigate the issues specific to staying connected in the bedroom and the disconnect going on in our spirit? That is the question.

First, I challenge you to see marriage from God's perspective. It is a union of a man and a woman for a lifetime. It offers security and intimacy:

> The husband should fulfill his marital duty to his wife, and likewise the wife to her husband. The wife's body does not belong to her alone but also to her husband. In the same way, the husband's body does not belong to

him alone but also to his wife. Do not deprive each other except by mutual consent and for a time, so that you may devote yourselves to prayer. Then come together again so that Satan will not tempt you because of your lack of self-control (1 Cor. 7:3-5).

Lovemaking is a gift from God; one in which a man and woman share intimacy with one another. Mutual pleasure and enjoyment is at its center. It's also an opportunity to bless our husband physically, emotionally and spiritually and to let him know that we desire him. It's exciting to a man to know his wife desires him. Physical love offers a man and a woman a chance to be part of something unique, something that belongs only to each other, a private treasure stored in our heart.

Second, I challenge you to decide to just do it. Do you know what the most important sex organ is in the human body? It's our brain. Turn the passion on in the brain, and the body will follow. God's design, the giving of our body, is a normal and natural part of marriage. Withholding sex or using sex as a bargaining chip doesn't fit the definition of loving our spouse as described in 1 Corinthians 13. And the Lord is clear that abstaining from sex is done only by mutual consent and done only to devote oneself to prayer.

The frequency of sexual intercourse is also something a couple must discover together, so communication between spouses is vital. Talking with our husband about bedroom expectations is a must.

Pleasurable sex is God's purpose. Have fun and make it good for your spouse. Make the effort. Did you know that mystery and anticipation are forms of foreplay? Do the setup—be part of it. If you've made plans for an interlude that night, spend the day thinking about your husband. Send him private messages that you're thinking about him. Give him hints about your plans. Be creative. Build anticipation. Make sure you're the only one on his mind.

Third, I challenge you to pray. Cover your love life with the power of God. Pray over your marriage bed. This starts before you even hit the bedroom. Pray for God to provide special times for you and your spouse to be alone and for that time to be protected. The marriage bed is sacred. Do not let anything interfere with that. Keep in mind that this is a chance to bless your husband and a way to connect with him.

When You Don't Agree

However, how do we connect with our spouse in the bedroom when his view of sex is different from God's perspective? What do we do if what our husband wants to do in the bedroom makes us uncomfortable?

The answer is communication. It is okay to have boundaries in the bedroom and in marriage in general. Every healthy relationship exists within established boundaries. So talk. Get counseling if need be. I recommend reading *Boundaries in Marriage* by Dr. Henry Cloud and Dr. John Townsend. An intimate and healthy love life is a key to loving for a lifetime.

As for what to do if your unbelieving spouse fears that you will become a prude in the bedroom because you're a Christian, reassurance is the key. Let him know that he is the only man in your world. Intimacy is a great way to reassure your husband that his place in your life is secure.

I realize that we are only touching the surface of this facet of marriage. I also don't pretend to have it all figured out, but I do know that a great sex life makes for a fantastic marriage. As the only believer in my marriage, my faith and understanding of God's design have made our love life better, sweeter, more fun and more fulfilling than I ever thought possible.

Intimacy, love, sex, trust, forgiveness, commitment, respect—all of these are components of married love and are gifts from the Lord. Enjoy!

Discovery

This may likely be a difficult chapter for you, so pray now and ask the Lord to show you one area in your life where a change will draw you closer to your spouse.

1. Think of a time in your marriage where you made an effort to connect with your husband that was outside of your comfort zone. What were the results?

2. What are two or three things you can do to reach out and connect with your spouse?

3. What attributes do you most admire about your husband? Write a list, take it with you each morning and give thanks to the Lord for him.

4. What is one area in which you can make an effort to enrich your bedroom connection?

5. What is one area of your intimacy that you will commit to prayer?

Pray

*O Lord, today I ask Your hand upon me to help me live out
1 Corinthians 13. Let this passage become alive in me.
Help me to wear kindness and patience, so my spouse will see
You in my eyes. Lord, help me to fiercely protect our love*

*from temptation and the efforts of the enemy. Help me to be
considerate and forgiving. Also, Lord, show me how to
connect with my husband. Show me where and how to
participate in his life. Allow me to give of myself in intimacy
so that it draws my husband and me closer together.
I ask Your grace and protection over our marriage. Let my
husband feel loved and may it move him closer to You.
In Jesus' powerful name, amen.*

Know the Essentials of Love: Hope, Joy, Peace and Trust (Oh, Yeah, and Respect)

(Dineen)

This is a profound mystery—but I am talking about Christ and the church.
However, each one of you also must love his wife as he loves himself,
and the wife must respect her husband.

EPHESIANS 5:32-33

He Needs Respect; She Needs Love

One day I sat in my car at a traffic light and prayed about my marriage, specifically about respecting my husband. God had placed this subject on my heart like a slow-building pressure cooker until I had to face it, front and center. I wasn't giving my husband the respect that I should.

I told God that I would seek my husband's forgiveness for not respecting him, if that's what needed to be done. Now I don't hear God that often, not like this, but He was pretty clear this particular day. Our dialogue went a little something like this:

"Lord, if You want me to tell him I'm sorry, I will. I'll seek his forgiveness, if that's what You think I should do."

"Would you even hesitate if he were a Christian?"

Ouch. Confession time. "No."

"Then why do you treat him any differently now? Treat him as if he were a Christian."

Needless to say, that conversation smarted a bit. And I did go to my husband and tell him I was sorry. My admission seemed to confuse him at first, but it did prompt him to ask me why I felt the need to apologize. I told him honestly that God had put it upon my heart to seek his forgiveness.

Thus my journey to understand how God wanted me to respect my husband began and led me to read several marriage books written from a Christian perspective. Interestingly enough, they all seemed to have a common thread: respect.

Men need respect and some even equate respect with love. Women, however, definitely go for the love first and need it in order to feel secure in marriage. And this does not mean the occasional "I love you" phrase thrown out randomly. We want to know we are the only woman who can make the heart of our man beat faster. The key here is security—not material security, but the security that comes from the reassurance that we are truly loved and desired by our man and that our place in his life is secure.

I wanted to see if some of what I'd read actually applied to my unequally yoked situation. What I read in Ephesians 5:32-33 fascinated me because it separated the roles of love and respect between the husband and wife, so I decided to do a little investigating myself through hands-on research. Basically, I put into action what I'd read and what I sensed God showing me.

At the time, our financial picture was intense. In the past, I would have expressed my worry and would have even made suggestions to push my husband in a specific direction. This time, I decided I would be the pillar by his side and show him I trusted his judgment completely to handle our financial situation. This was not easy for me. I've never been one to bite my tongue, but I do tend to clench my jaw. Let's just say, my jaw stayed pretty sore throughout this period.

I could not have done this without God's leading and strength. I amazed even myself, but I knew my actions affirmed my husband's role as the leader of our household and showed him I believed we would be fine.

Amazing things happened. Instead of the stressful situation putting us at odds with one another, we grew closer—even to the point that my husband would send me messages on my phone or computer to tell me he loved or missed me. (He hadn't done that in quite a while.)

The more I aligned myself with him as I sensed God calling me to do, and the more I showed my husband that I respected his decisions and trusted him, the more my husband drew closer to me. A whole new realm of truth opened up to me.

I know this isn't easy and, as I said, I don't think I could have done this without God's strength. No, I *know* I couldn't have. My way would have been to nag, worry and add to the stress of the situation. But God showed me that by doing this His way, I honored and respected not only my husband but God as well. And let me tell you, nothing is more exciting, invigorating and peaceful than obedience to God's will. I had peace in the middle of an impending storm.

Our Deepest Needs

I am my beloved's, and his desire is for me.
SONG OF SOLOMON 7:10, *ESV*

We see it in movies and books. The woman goes into the world, convinced she has a soulmate out there somewhere. She'll go from man to man, until she finds the right one. Unfortunately for our heroine, each man takes her farther and farther away from a true love relationship. She's become the victim of a trap that many women fall into.

Most of us grew up thinking that there is only one person in the world who will meet all our needs. And when our marriage fails or when we're not happy, we question our marriage choice.

I know I grew up believing this lie, and I even bought into it during the early years of my marriage. When my husband didn't meet my needs, I wondered if I'd made a mistake. *Did I marry the wrong guy? What if my true soulmate is still out there, looking for me?*

Thinking this way is a lethal trap, deadly to a marriage and destructive to the heart of our unsuspecting man who hasn't a clue about our misconceptions. Can't you just see the question mark sprouting from your husband's head?

We actually do have this desire for our deepest needs to be met by the one most important to us. The mistake too many of us make is in seeking this from a person and not from the God who created us to need Him. God designed us with a need for deep love—to be seen and acknowledged, treasured and appreciated; to be known and understood on the deepest of levels. We can't possibly expect our husbands to fulfill that need 100 percent of the time without fail.

But we often do.

When we seek this from our husband, we are putting god-like expectations on an incapable human being. Our husband can't possibly fulfill this need, and he'll wind up feeling like a failure when he tries. And we end up feeling unloved, undesired and resentful. This resentment then creeps in and threatens the marriage relationship.

Instead, God wants us to look to Him for those needs. When our expectations are rightly placed in the One who created those needs in the first place, we discover a freedom in our marriage that allows us to be the woman God created each of us to be and the wife He needs us to be so that He can work through us to reach our husband. The burden is taken off our man, as is the label of failure. We can then respect our husband as he is and love him unconditionally.

How do we love our man unconditionally? First John 4 is one of the most powerful books of the Bible about God's love. You can read that book over and over again and still not completely grasp just how deeply God loves us. The key, though, is right in verse 19, a verse quoted by Lynn in the previous chapter:

We love because he first loved us (1 John 4:19).

Let that truth wrap around your brain, and truly accept it. Then and only then will it reach the depths of your heart and that deepest of needs. It may take time, but to truly love unconditionally requires us to comprehend that we are loved unconditionally by God. This is a turning point to understanding true love (sacrificial love) and the beginning of loving and respecting our husband through God's strength, not our own.

It's Not About Us

Therefore, since we are surrounded by such a great cloud of witnesses, let us throw off everything that hinders and the sin that so easily entangles, and let us run with perseverance the race marked out for us.

HEBREWS 12:1

If you are like me, you have prayed for weeks, days, months, perhaps even years for your spouse's salvation. The prayers now, however, aren't as frequent as before. Instead, a sense of hopelessness has slowly replaced the original fervency of your petitions. You've asked so many times, yet God seems to either not hear you or your spouse has an unusually thick skull. Nothing's getting through. I can only say one thing: Don't stop now.

While living in Europe, I was part of a small support group for unequally yoked women. For one of our monthly sessions, our small-group leader did a wonderful thing: She planned a meeting with six female guests who were once unequally yoked. Each of the six women shared her journey as an unequally yoked spouse, including the pièce de résistance: how her spouse had come to Christ and where he stood as of that day.

I remember one woman sharing how her young daughter wound up influencing her husband to make the all-important decision to become a Christian. Others spoke of life-changing events playing a significant role. One woman mentioned the 12 years she waited, praying for her husband to accept Christ. Twelve years.

I recall thinking, *That won't be me.* Little did I know then that my years would exceed hers.

The one thread that ran through all their testimonies was prayer. Keep praying, keep believing, and then pray some more. Prayer is the key ingredient here, but how do we keep going when we see nothing change? How do we persevere when the enemy's whispering things in our ear?

"He'll never change, so why bother?"

"You blew up at him yesterday. What kind of witness can you possibly offer?"

"It's hopeless. There's nothing you can do."

I'll admit, I haven't always prayed consistently for my husband; but since God told me my husband was my Jericho and that I was to march around him in prayer, I've stuck to a weekly prayer schedule to keep me on track.

Have I seen any change since then? No.

Have I witnessed a softening of my husband's heart toward God? No.

Have I quit praying? No.

At one point, God grabbed my attention again and told me to step things up: more prayer, more marching, daily, keep it going. Why? I don't know. Maybe the battle for my husband's soul was more intense at the time. What I do know is that God is big enough to just snap His fingers and make it happen. He knows my prayer before I even speak it. So why more, why now?

Because I wasn't ready.

Feel free to read that line again. It surprised me when I wrote it.

Go back to the time you started praying for your spouse. Spend a little time there and look at who you were then. Now come back to the present and answer this question: Are you the same person now that you were then?

I'm betting you said no. (If not, then we really need to talk!) You may not see any changes in your husband, or perhaps you see some miniscule movement in the right direction, but I'm guessing you've changed significantly. The road has been rough, full of potholes, but each time you bounced through one of those setbacks, you wound up stronger, better able to handle the next difficulty in the road.

Prayer is truly a journey. When we open our heart and align our will with God's, we can't help but be transformed. God is just that way. Even when our prayers seem to ricochet like rubber balls, He's there, helping us pitch the next throw.

The point is to keep pitching, keep praying. Don't give up. Don't let the enemy win. God wants us to have the best arm possible so that when that day comes—that amazing day when our spouse says yes to Jesus—we've got the muscle to help him walk his own journey of prayer and faith.

To Know and Be Known

But the man who loves God is known by God.

1 CORINTHIANS 8:3

One day as I wrote down a prayer, the ache in my heart formed into five words: "to know and be known." Baffled by its meaning, yet fearful of the ramifications, I realized that this was one of my deepest needs and something I wanted desperately in my marriage. I thought if my husband shared my faith, he would truly know who I was.

"To know and be known."

What's at the heart of this plea-like desire? If you're like me, your faith defines who you are. At your very core, you find God, and everything you do is affected by this relationship.

Now I don't say this to appear more than I am. Believe me when I say that the closer I come to Christ, the more I see how truly fallen I am. No, this goes deeper. It goes to a deep need to share ourselves with our Creator and with our husband.

But here's our dilemma: How do we share our authentic self when the very essence that defines us is a Creator our husband refuses to acknowledge? We already struggle with who we are in a society that tells us we're not good enough, no matter what we do. Our marriage is supposed to be a place where we can be our true self, secure in the knowledge that we are loved and accepted. But what happens when what we believe is unacceptable to the one we've committed to spend our life with? Let's look at this in two parts:

1. "To know." I want to know and understand my spouse, to relate to him on a spiritual level. Yet our mismatch makes this virtually impossible. I can't know him this way, because he is still entrenched in his worldly state. The spirit I long to connect with isn't there. But to

delve deeper is to understand that who I truly long to know is God—to understand my place in His kingdom and to find peace in this knowledge.

2. "And be known." I want my husband to know who I am, to understand that my faith defines who I am at the very core of my being. Again I am drawn to connect with him on this spiritual level. To look further is to see a deep-seated need to be known by God. To know I matter to Him. That I am more than just one of many and unique in the Master's eye.

Our natural tendency is to search for fulfillment of our greatest needs in the ones we are closest to: our husband, our children, our friends, our ministries, our jobs. Yet God desires that He be the One we turn to for this deep fulfillment and connection. This is the essence of our relationship with Him—our one true love. And He's the One who placed this desire within us to point us right back to Him.

I can't relate to what it feels like to be married to a believer. I can only imagine it, picture it, desire it—deeply yearn for and even dream about it. I'm guessing you feel the same. But therein lies a question we have to ask ourselves at some point: *Do I want my husband's salvation more than I want Jesus?*

Anything in our lives that becomes more important than our relationship with God is an idol. And we can so easily make an idol out of our husband's salvation, desiring it more than even our own relationship with God.

Part of this goes back to what I said in the previous section about not being ready. Our husband is not the only one God is working on. He's changing us, too—preparing us. Why? So that when our husband finally takes this step, we aren't tempted to seek him to fill this need instead of God. As much as we want our husband to know Jesus, God wants us to know Him first and foremost.

And if you've walked with God long enough and read the Bible, you know how He feels about idols. He will not tolerate them because He knows what we really need is so much better than what we think we want. My experience has proven this truth time and again.

Amazingly, when we put God first in our lives, our deepest needs are met. Oftentimes, the met needs are ones we didn't even know we had. And the beauty of it all? In God's presence, we are known from head to toe—our thoughts, our needs and even our dreams.

God Is the Wild Hope Maker

Now faith is being sure of what we hope for and
certain of what we do not see.
HEBREWS 11:1

So how do we keep hoping—and praying—when everything we see tells us that there is no hope? And how do we go beyond our own earthly hope and experience God's wild hope?

According to Hebrews 11:1, the very definition of faith is being sure of what we hope for and certain of what we do not see. But how do we apply that to situations that leave us feeling hopeless, as if our prayers are unheard and unanswered? So often we see the struggle of being unequally yoked as a battle for us to simply hang on to our own faith. In the midst of the adversity the mismatched marriage naturally brings, we find ourselves praying and hoping for our husband's salvation. Day after day we petition God. Months or even years pass with no visible change.

As I became more involved in this ministry to the unequally yoked, and as my own family was hit by an unexpected trial that turned our lives upside down, this became my main question to God: How do we continue to hope and persevere in prayer? I searched my concordance and found one principle Scripture that for me shed a high-focus light beam on this dimly lit subject:

> Even youths grow tired and weary, and young men stumble and fall; but those who hope in the LORD will renew their strength. They will soar on wings like eagles; they will run and not grow weary, they will walk and not be faint (Isa. 40:30-31).

The key seems to be in the third line ("those who hope in the LORD"). Could it be that we place our hope in the transformation we so desperately desire in our spouse and not in the author of our faith, Jesus? Are we looking in the wrong direction?

When we keep our eyes on our situation and our unbelieving spouse, how can we possibly continue to hope, let alone have wild hope? The burden of unfulfilled desire becomes the object of attention and saps the strength we need. The burden is too heavy for us to carry, because we've switched from relying on God's strength to depending on our own very limited supply.

When do you feel as if you can't go any farther because you have no more strength left? When you've prayed over and over again for your husband to believe in Christ? When you've prayed over and over for a child to be healed? For a job? For a difficult situation to find a peaceful solution? For a loved one to come back to you?

Now ask yourself this question: *What am I waiting on?* Did you answer that you are waiting on:

· Your spouse to come to faith?
· Your child to be healthy again?

· The right job to come your way?
· This situation to be fixed and go away?
· Your loved one to come home?

Now go back and ask yourself, *Who am I waiting for?* If those who hope in the Lord will be strengthened, then by keeping your hope firmly placed in God (the only One who has the power to bring your husband to belief), you can persevere and continue, even when things appear utterly hopeless.

With God we can soar above the murky waters of hopelessness. With God we can rise above our own limited ability, and we can trust completely in a God bigger and stronger than anything we are dealing with, even the most stubborn of men. With God we can have wild hope—the kind that perseveres even when someone asks you, "How can you be so sure?"

I know my God. I believe my God. I hope in my God. He can do anything. We can choose to believe this completely. When we keep our eyes focused on God and place the burden of proof, so to speak, on Him, we are free to walk in a hope that is not of this world.

It's God's wild hope.

The Glue to Hope, Joy and Peace

May the God of hope fill you with all joy and peace as you
trust in him, so that you may overflow with hope
by the power of the Holy Spirit.

ROMANS 15:13

One day I wrote this verse on an index card in the most delicious shade of pink. (How could I miss it?) I love picking apart God's Word. I've found that just about everything in the Bible has at least two layers, or two meanings. Isn't that just like God? Nothing lost and everything to gain. He wastes nothing and redeems everything.

In reading this verse over and over again, two things stood out to me. The first thing was that God is "the God of hope," which tells us that just as Christ is the author of our faith, He is also the creator of our hope. We can't manufacture hope by our own ability. If we're to truly know a hope that endures, we must pray and let God do what He does best.

The second thing that stood out was "overflow with the hope by the power of the Holy Spirit," which affirms what we're told in the first part of the verse. Again, it's only by God's power that we not only know hope but also overflow with it. I don't know about you, but knowing that the hope I want most will come from God and not from me lifted a weight off my shoulders. Yet another thing I don't have to strive to accomplish. (Whew!)

Now the deeper layer (or the creamy filling, if you prefer) in this hope-filled nugget: In reading the Bible, I found one word that is constantly used in association with hope and faith. If you guessed "trust," you're exactly right. Look at the verse again. God tells us that *He* will fill us with joy and peace as we trust in Him so that we can overflow with hope (meaning that you must have one in order to accomplish the other).

Joy, peace and hope can't exist where trust is lacking.

Our trials are designed to bring us to a place of complete and total trust in God. No, this process won't be completed until we join our Lord and Savior in the heavenly realms, but our time here on earth is about preparation for what's to come. (That's what I tell my daughters when they get frustrated with the here and now—it's just a blip on their eternal lifeline.)

So if you're struggling to find hope, trust in the fact that we serve an ever-faithful God; and call out to Him to restore, renew and build your hope. Write Romans 15:13 down and pray it every day. Replace each "you" with "me" or "I." This is a vital weapon in the battle for our faith, our hope, and our unbelieving husband. God didn't just give us His Word to read. He gave it to us to use—

to learn from and to grow on and for battle and protection.

Finally, the most precious layer of all (like I said, God wastes nothing and redeems everything): God has absolutely everything we need. He planned it that way. He never intended for us to walk this path alone. He's right there, waiting for us to ask for His help. Or we can just sit at His feet and bask in His glory.

Or we can pray verses written on bright pink index cards.

Discovery

You're getting close to experiencing wild hope in your marriage, so don't stop now! Ask God to open your eyes and heart to hear His truth and promises as you work through the discussion questions.

1. Think about your husband. Do you respect him in the way that God is asking you to respect him?

2. What deep needs are you expecting your husband to meet? Write down each one, and then pray and seek God for fulfillment (or release) of these needs.

3. Rate your prayer life on a scale of 1 to 10, with 1 being "I pitch an occasional prayer" and 10 being "I pray until I'm blue in the face." (If you wrote "10," I definitely want a picture!) Even when you don't see immediate results, do you keep praying? If not, what can you do to build those prayer muscles? Be specific.

4. Draw three columns on a sheet of paper. In the first column, make a list of your unanswered prayers. Examine each one prayerfully, asking God to reveal anything you need to do, change or accept in regard to each one. In the second column, write down who or

what you have placed your hope in for each prayer. Read Hebrews 12:2. How can you make a prayer out of this verse, telling God you will keep your eyes on Jesus for each concern or issue? Write down your prayer and make a commitment to God to follow through as He leads you. (We'll fill in the third column after you read chapter 10.)

5. How hard is it for you to trust God for the salvation of your husband? Do you trust God to equip you with everything you need to thrive in your spiritual mismatch?

6. Look up Ecclesiastes 3:11. God's Word says He makes everything beautiful in His time—not ours. This verse also tells us that God set eternity in the hearts of men. Do you believe this to be true of your husband? Create a prayer for your spouse, using this verse to ask God to awaken a longing to know God and His eternity in your husband's heart.

Prayer

Lord Jesus, be the author and perfecter of my faith.
Be the source of an enduring hope planted deep within me
and overflowing to Your glory. If I have looked to my
husband to fulfill a need designed to be filled by You,
forgive me and show me how to seek Your fulfillment,
Lord, for You are my portion and everything I really need.
Help me to understand that truth.

Lord, You know my struggles and weaknesses. You know the
heartache I face on a daily basis. You know how I struggle

some days just to keep going. Help me to remember that I can draw strength—strength that does not run out—from You and only You. Holy Spirit, alert me when I make that subtle shift from God's strength to my own.

And lastly, Lord, give me a wild hope to not only persevere but also to truly thrive in my marriage and leave the results to You. In Jesus' precious name, amen.

Believe Your Marriage Is Blessed

(Dineen)

"For this reason a man will leave his father and mother and be united to his wife, and the two will become one flesh." So they are no longer two, but one. Therefore what God has joined together, let man not separate.

MARK 10:7–9

The Way to Mismatchdom

"How did we get here?" is the question we all dance around. The one we sometimes want to ask but don't. The one we dread when asked of us. The one we know the person's dying to ask us when we tell them that our spouse doesn't share our faith.

"Did you know he wasn't a Christian when you married him?"

I can hear the universal cringe. Believe me, I know. Been there, done that, a dozen times at least. I don't mind the question when it comes out of genuine concern—someone in need of understanding for his or her own situation or for a friend or loved one. It's when I hear the judgment playing peek-a-boo as a question that takes me right back to the guilt.

For years I had good answers for this question. I had all kinds of ways to say "I had no idea what he was" without making myself look bad. But does it really matter?

In Matthew 6:34, Jesus tells us not to worry about tomorrow. He has our future covered if we trust in Him. With this being true, why would this great big God of grace want us to dwell on the past when He sent His Son to take care of it?

We don't have to live in the shadows, lurking behind a shield of shame. This is not what God wants for us. He's calling us, no matter how we arrived here, to be the presence of Christ in our husbands' lives. And I don't mean browbeating him with a Bible or with our "Christianese." I mean living our lives in obedience to Christ—obeying His call to act or not to act, to speak or not to speak. Many times Jesus spoke the loudest through His silence. He knew how to read and speak between the lines.

Do not let the enemy weigh you down with guilt over a decision of the past to marry your unbelieving spouse. Confession frees the spirit, literally. Regardless if you knowingly or unknowingly married an unbeliever, confess your error, accept God's forgiveness, and move forward. God will still bless your marriage. My marriage is a walking, talking testimony to this truth.

Shame and condemnation are tools the enemy will use to great advantage to diminish or even prevent our witness. And that cloak of shame can't exist while we are sporting our shield of faith—part of the armor of God (see Eph. 6:10-12). In chapter 10, we will take a detailed look at this passage and how it is lived out in our unique marriage, but here, the point I want you to understand is that we have no reason to feel shame or condemnation for our choice of a husband.

The Call to Obedience

Later I passed by, and when I looked at you and saw that you were old enough for love, I spread the corner of my garment over you and covered your nakedness. I gave you my solemn oath and entered into a covenant with you, declares the Sovereign Lord, and you became mine.

EZEKIEL 16:8

One evening, my oldest daughter surprised me by pulling out our old family videos. The first one she popped into the machine was, of course, the wedding video.

I don't think I'd viewed the footage for a good 15 years. We marveled at how young her dad and I looked and how much the styles had changed in 20 years. (Hey, it was the eighties!)

As the video played, my husband arrived home from work and joined us in my daughter's room. At this stage in the video, the ceremony was at the point when the pastor instructed us to repeat our vows, and he prayed—a lot. I honestly didn't remember the wedding being so steeped in prayer and verse. As we watched, I wondered what my husband was thinking as he saw himself as a very young man bow his head and recite the Lord's Prayer. Needless to say, I observed myself as a young woman do the very same thing, and I realized how little I knew God at the time.

One part of the ceremony struck me especially: The pastor spoke of marriage as a covenant and that ours would be blessed if we lived in obedience to God. If anything, I've learned over the years just how important obedience is. And I'm still learning this, to be perfectly honest.

But exactly what is God calling us to do in our unequally yoked situations? Is He asking us to do anything different from what He would do in an equally yoked covenant relationship? The Old Testament repeatedly mentions the covenant God made with His people, Israel. The very first thing He required of the Israelites was their commitment to put Him above everything else. He was to be first and foremost in their lives:

> Hear, O Israel: The LORD our God, the LORD is one. Love the LORD your God with all your heart and with all your soul and with all your strength (Deut. 6:4-5).

What God requires of all covenant relationships, including marriages, is that He be at the center. Whether your husband believes this or not doesn't matter. This is the obedience God requires of us and is a major key to thriving in a spiritually unequal marriage. When our eyes are focused on God, our circumstances stay where they belong—in His most capable hands.

God's Plan for Your Marriage

And we know that in all things God works for the good of those who love him, who have been called according to his purpose.

ROMANS 8:28

The longer I walk this journey with God, the more I've come to realize that everything has a purpose. God is not wasteful. He uses every detail of our lives—the good and the bad—to bring about His purpose. As I shared earlier, God laid claim to my life at a very young age. And now, at the midway point of my life, I can look back and see parts of the puzzle coming together.

I can say without a doubt that God put my husband in my life at this particular time to fulfill His purpose. Did I know this in the beginning? No. Did I know this when my husband finally told me he'd decided that he was an atheist? No. Do I know what the result of God's purpose will be in my mismatched marriage? No, but I'm willing to trust Him to the end and find out. Like reading a good book, I'm hooked now and have to finish the story, and God is the best author I know. His endings never disappoint.

> In the same way, the Spirit helps us in our weakness. We do not know what we ought to pray for, but the Spirit himself intercedes for us with groans that words cannot express. And he who searches our hearts knows the mind of the Spirit, because the Spirit intercedes for the saints in accordance with God's will (Rom. 8:26-27).

I can tell you this Scripture is true, because I've heard these moanings. The night my husband shared his choice to be an atheist was probably one of the most painful times in my life. The physical sensation resembled a punch in the stomach, and the emotional one . . . well, I can only describe it as utter despair. I couldn't even pray, nor did I know what to pray.

I look back even now and believe that part of what I felt was the Spirit's reaction to my husband's words. Perhaps that's why God allowed me to hear the Holy Spirit this one time, to comfort me in my pain and to be clear that He understood my suffering because He had suffered too. From that day forward, I had to rely on God to rebuild my marriage according to His design, not my expectations.

God has blessed my marriage and honored my obedience to Him, my commitment to my marriage, and my determination to honor my husband. But I know that more challenges are coming and that my marriage will become a true image of what God intended. Watching the old wedding video was like God saying, "See, I've been there all along. Just wait and see what I do next."

The amazing thing is, despite the fact that my beliefs and my husband's beliefs are different, God still blesses our marriage, just as He blesses a marriage between believers. He is faithful and honors the covenant of marriage, even if you're unequally yoked. The key is to remember that God wants your spouse saved even more than you do. God loves us this much—all of us.

Biblical Truths

But thanks be to God, who always leads us in triumphal procession in Christ and through us spreads everywhere the fragrance of the knowledge of him. For we are to God the aroma of Christ among those who are being saved and those who are perishing. To the one we are the smell of death; to the other, the fragrance of life. And who is equal to such a task?

2 CORINTHIANS 2:14-16

The verses above reveal several treasures. Roman triumphal processions were known for the use of incense as treasures and captives were paraded for all to see. For the victors, this aroma meant sweet triumph; for the captives, slavery and death. Paul used this analogy to represent the aroma of Christ. To believers, it is the sweet smell of mercy and salvation. To unbelievers, it's the stench of death.

We are called to be the aroma of Christ in our marriage, and by simply living our faith as best we can, this naturally happens. But here's where it gets tricky: At times we will be as sweet incense to our husband, a welcome fragrance. At other times, our faith will be a painful reminder to his soul of what's missing. I believe this is part of the unseen battle in which God calls us to wear our armor. We will meet opposition as we pray for our husband's salvation.

However, the real nugget in these verses is "those who are being saved." God showed me this one day and put an intense excitement in my heart. The verb tense is present and ongoing and has a fascinating implication: Salvation is a process, and it's one we don't always see.

During our time in Switzerland, God used the story of Jericho to show me that I needed to march around my husband in prayer. At one point God gave me three words when I prayed for my husband's salvation: "So be it." This was the beginning of the salvation process for my husband, one that is still in the works. I can't see anything significant happening, nor do I see any change in him. But I know God set into motion a process that will one day culminate in my husband's salvation:

> But if the unbeliever leaves, let him do so. A believing man or woman is not bound in such circumstances; God has called us to live in peace. How do you know, wife, whether you will save your husband? Or, how do you know, husband, whether you will save your wife? Nevertheless, each one should retain the place in life

that the Lord assigned to him and to which God has called him. This is the rule I lay down in all the churches (1 Cor. 7:15-17).

Paul didn't say in these verses that we have a way out. On the contrary, he told us the opposite. As the believing spouse, we are encouraged to live in peace and make our marriage work (but not to deny our faith nor to endure abuse).

According to Paul, God may have put us where we are because we are to be a key factor to our spouse's salvation. We may be one of the tools God is choosing specifically to use in bringing our loved one to Him. God may have called us to this exact place at this exact time.

As I said earlier, I know now that God put my husband in my life at a particular time to fulfill His purpose. And what I'm coming to realize is that God placed me in my husband's life for a purpose as well. The closer I come to the time of my husband's salvation, the more I've discovered I'm part of this process. And like Christ, my actions, my support and my unconditional love speak the loudest to my dear husband.

We are truly the aroma—stinky or sweet—of Christ in our spouse's life, And we are also the vessel in which God will bring His blessings. Believe it.

Blessed Doesn't Mean Easy

No, in all these things we are more than conquerors through him who loved us.

ROMANS 8:37

In the fall of 2008, our 14-year-old daughter was diagnosed with a malignant brain tumor. Like most parents, we never imagined something like this could happen to us. Our lives were suddenly thrust into a narrow focus of hospitals, doctors, surgeries and treatments. Praise God, today she is cancer free and in complete recovery. Physically.

What we didn't expect was the emotional fallout that compounded an already existing condition of depression and teenage angst. At times, the first months—going through all her surgeries, radiation treatments and even an ER run one panicked evening—seemed easier than the emotional trials she would endure. If you're a parent, you know the pain of watching your child struggle. I heard Beth Moore once say of mothers that we're only as happy as our saddest child.[1] Her words ring true, don't they?

We can easily allow ourselves to see only the moment of despair and not the blessings and hope God holds constantly ready in His hand for our benefit. I have to remind myself on the worst of days that it's not the true picture of what will be, because I know God's working. The next week, the next day, even the next hour could present a completely different picture.

Our trials and hardships are unique to who we are and are uniquely designed to challenge and try us, even push us to the very edges of our faith. God's Word not only tells us this but also shares the benefit:

> Not only so, but we also rejoice in our sufferings, because we know that suffering produces perseverance; perseverance, character; and character, hope. And hope does not disappoint us, because God has poured out his love into our hearts by the Holy Spirit, whom he has given us (Rom. 5:3-5).

Our human nature pushes us toward the easy way, the less treacherous path. But then we find ourselves left in the trenches without a view of the sun breaking on a dark horizon. We miss the revelation and blessing of God's faithfulness and hope, and we find our world limited to the muck surrounding us.

However, our spirit desires to tackle the rough uphill terrain because it instinctively knows the promise that's waiting to be discovered over the next ridge. It knows without a doubt that God is there waiting to welcome us into deeper intimacy with Him.

The most profound thing that God has ever shared with me in our struggle to bring our family to wholeness were these words: "There is purpose in your pain." These words weren't easy to hear at first, and I won't tell you what I told Him (thank goodness God loves me despite my temper tantrums). But I recognized the truth and grabbed on to it for dear life.

Why? Because to think we go through such struggles and heartbreak in life for no reason at all is completely intolerable to my sense of justice and purpose. If I am to suffer, let it at least be for the benefit of someone, if not myself. When we choose to persevere for God because He deems it important to our future and quite possibly to the salvation of our husband, we can trust in God's faithfulness. He will bless us and our marriage for our faithfulness to Him.

The trials in a spiritually mismatched marriage can be intense, but there is comfort in knowing that God only allows us to struggle for good reasons. It's like the story of Hananiah, Mishael and Azariah (Shadrach, Meshach and Abednego) in Daniel 3. These three men were willing to perish in the fires of persecution in order to stand firm in their faith in God. They told Nebuchadnezzar that their God would save them, and that even if He didn't, they would die before worshiping a false god. They persevered, and God rewarded them for their faithfulness. They didn't die, their untouched clothing didn't even smell like smoke, and they experienced the presence of God in a most tangible and visible form (see Dan.

3:25). They walked out of the fiery furnace a true testimony to their God and their faith—a rich blessing indeed.

Sometimes our mismatched marriages (and our trials) can feel like that fiery furnace. But like Shadrach, Meshach and Abednego, we're not alone. God is in the middle of it with us. The choice is ours whether we come out stronger in our faith and present a powerful witness to those watching, like Nebuchadnezzar (our husbands), or if we come out smelling like smoke (bitter and resentful).[2]

The key is to stop seeing our mismatched marriage and our husband as problems to be solved and accept both as blessings to be enjoyed. We can learn from our struggles and grow in faith. God wants to show us the beauty present in our situation and to teach us not to be afraid to get our hands dirty in order to sift for the jewels awaiting discovery. He nudges us to climb the treacherous mountain so we can see the sun peeking over a horizon filled with promise. He wants us to know that we will find His presence even in the darkest of places.

This is where we experience joy in the midst of trial. We discover the ability to laugh and appreciate special moments despite imperfect conditions, and, most importantly, we learn that we are not responsible for the results. God is. And that's when we discover our greatest blessing—God Himself. He is our portion and our great reward. You can't find better treasure than that.

Discovery

One of the most difficult truths to accept in our faith is that God allows trials in our lives for our good and for the good of others. Ask God to prepare and open your heart to work through the next set of questions, so you can find peace and understanding.

1. Reflect on how you entered your marriage. Do you still have regrets or carry guilt for marrying your spouse? If so, seek God's forgiveness or His peace, and allow Him to bring healing to your heart and to your marriage.

2. Do you view your marriage as a covenant blessed by God? Pray and ask God to show you how He has blessed your marriage, and then make a list of those blessings and review it frequently.

3. Is there any area of your marriage in which you feel you aren't being obedient to God? If so, what steps do you need to take to change this? Be specific.

4. Do you believe the promise of Romans 8:28? If so, can you see some of God's purpose in your situation? If not, what keeps you from believing God is working for your good as well as the good of your husband?

5. In what ways do you feel you are the aroma of Christ for your spouse?

6. What struggles are you facing right now? What do you think God is trying to teach you?

Prayer

Precious Lord, You are my great Redeemer. Please forgive my unbelief and help me to truly believe my marriage is blessed. Help me to release the burdens of the past into Your hands and find freedom in Your merciful love.

Lord, teach me the kind of obedience You are calling me to in my marriage. Help me to be the aroma of Christ to my spouse. Be my strength in the midst of whatever life brings. In the holy and blessed name of Christ, amen.

Notes

1. Beth Moore, *Esther: It's Tough Being a Woman,* video series (Nashville, TN: LifeWay Press, 2008).
2. Beth Moore, *Daniel: Lives of Integrity, Words of Prophecy—Member Book* (Nashville, TN: LifeWay Press, 2006), p. 47.

Trade Perfection for Authenticity

(Dineen)

He [the Lord] said to me, "My grace is sufficient for you, for my power is made perfect in weakness." Therefore I will boast all the more gladly about my weaknesses, so that Christ's power may rest on me.

2 CORINTHIANS 12:9

A Fine Linen Belt

In Jeremiah 13:1, God told Jeremiah to purchase a linen belt and tie it around his waist. Jeremiah did as God had instructed. Then God spoke a second time and told Jeremiah to bury the belt in a crevice (see v. 4). Many days later, Jeremiah unearthed the belt at God's direction and found it "ruined and completely useless" (v. 7). God used this illustration to show Jeremiah what Judah and Israel had become in their idolatry—"useless."

As I read this chapter in Jeremiah, I sensed the Holy Spirit saying to me, "Stop and pay attention." Throughout the Bible, we usually see linen used in association with Christ and His priesthood, going all the way back to Exodus and Aaron. Revelation 19:8 says that "fine linen stands for the righteous acts of the saints."

Isn't it like God to use a metaphor to reflect His meaning on so many levels? Judah and Israel had lost their righteousness because of their pride, wickedness and stubbornness. They became as broken, tattered and "useless" as that linen belt.

God further expounds upon the meaning of the belt in Jeremiah 13:11:

> "For as a belt is bound around a man's waist, so I bound the whole house of Israel and the whole house of Judah to me," declares the LORD, "to be my people for my renown and praise and honor. But they have not listened."

See how the past tense is used when God says He "bound" the houses of Israel and Judah? God had already tied that belt, binding the two houses to Himself. Then, at the end, He switched to the present perfect tense: "But they have not listened to me." Starting in the past and continuing into the present, Judah's and Israel's unrighteousness had disintegrated the belt binding them to God.

Then I asked God to connect the dots for me—how did this relate to being unequally yoked? He gave me a picture of how the believing spouse can be that linen belt, a representation of righteousness (God's, not ours), binding the marriage to God. Yet if we hide our faith, the belt disintegrates and becomes useless.

Now I'm not saying we should beat our husbands over the head with Scripture or get preachy. Remember, the reference in Revelation referred to "righteous acts." I believe this described who they had become through the changing power of Christ. They simply lived as Christ called them to, letting their light shine before men (and women).

If you're like me, you've learned that pushing the gospel on someone unwilling to hear it is ineffective, but nothing can stop us from being a living representation of Christ in our homes each and every day. That doesn't mean being perfect. It means being authentic. What greater witness is there than a life changed and redeemed?

How is that most effective? Not by words but by acts!

We are called to be that linen belt in our day-to-day lives, but burying it will only make us ineffective, which is what the enemy desires most since he can't take away our salvation. We may not have the freedom to voice our religious beliefs in our homes, but we can live boldly as a saint through our actions, through the peace of knowing that Christ suffers with us and through the knowledge that God wants our loved one to know His Son even more than we do.

We can be that fine linen belt, unbroken and unblemished, strengthened and purified by the very God we love—and by the great intercession of our Savior, Jesus.

A Confession

Wives, in the same way be submissive to your husbands so that,
if any of them do not believe the word, they may be won over
without words by the behavior of their wives, when they see
the purity and reverence of your lives.
1 PETER 3:1-2

One night, I went out to dinner with my husband. As I was sitting there, I suddenly had this deep desire to confess something that had happened earlier in the day, something about which I still felt somewhat ashamed. Ever been in that place where the words are coming out and, in your mind, you're wondering what in the world is going on? What possessed you to even bring up such a thing?

So there I sat in this posh restaurant, enjoying an evening of peace, and I proceeded to tell my husband how I was rude to the receptionist at the doctor's office earlier that day.

I even told him, "I can make all kinds of excuses. I didn't want to be there. Was dreading it, in fact. The receptionist's greeting lacked any friendliness. Most likely due to the fact that she was flustered at the moment. She made me wait, and then she proceeded to help the next person who walked in."

Yada, yada, yada . . .

But still, she didn't deserve my attitude. That's it right there: my attitude.

The funny thing is, the situation at the doctor's office reminded me of someone else's rudeness I'd observed in years past and how uncomfortable it had made me to be a witness to it. To think I had treated someone in that manner mortified me. How could I have done that?

I shared this with my husband. All of it. Why? I have no idea, but I did. Me, the Christian, mistreated a stranger. What would he think of my faith now? What would he think of the Jesus I professed to follow?

Wait. It gets better.

I went on to tell my husband how I had prayed silently, asking God for an opportunity to apologize. (Yeah, I know. What was I thinking?) I went on to share that before I could even say "amen," this young woman was standing in front of me. Right in front of me.

I continued my story, "I told her flat out, I was sorry, that she didn't deserve my attitude. She said she understood the circumstances, but I told her I still shouldn't have treated her that way."

The Holy Spirit had to be sitting at the dinner table that night. I finished my story and looked at my husband. He smiled and said, "I bet she really appreciated that." But what stopped me was the subtext—the pride I saw in his eyes. I screwed up, and he was proud of me.

I still have no idea why I told him about what happened, but I do believe the Holy Spirit was at work that evening. Up to this point, I'd thought I had to be a perfect representation of what a Christian should be, but God exposed my flaws and my pride, and He continues to prune them away.

God doesn't want perfection. He wants authenticity.

Heart Tablets

You yourselves are our letter, written on our hearts, known and read by everybody. You show that you are a letter from Christ, the result of our ministry, written not with ink but with the Spirit of the living God, not on tablets of stone but on tablets of human hearts.

2 CORINTHIANS 3:2-3

If I could tell my husband one thing today, I would tell him that I love him. If I could speak special words to him today, I would speak of my love for him. If I could show him who I love most, I would show him Christ.

How do we show Christ? How do we convey with actions what we'd like to say with words? How can we show Christ and not just speak of Him? For the spiritually mismatched, this is our greatest challenge. More often than not, it's our actions that speak of our faith more effectively than our words.

I love the imagery Paul used in comparing tablets of stone to tablets of human hearts. He speaks of showing ourselves as messages from Christ so undeniable that we leave a permanent impression on the hearts of those we meet, on those we love.

That's a tall order to fulfill, but Paul made another point clear here: It is not by our efforts that we do this. If it were, we would be taking credit for another's salvation—as if we, by our own efforts, had saved them.

No, Paul referred directly to the Spirit of the living God. The Holy Spirit is the ink, the markings, the unforgettable and undeniable presence of God made visible with His Son through us. We are simply the parchment, a willing and ready surface for the Holy Spirit to make His mark.

We can find tremendous comfort and inspiration in this. I mean comfort in the sense that it isn't up to us to know what to say or how to say it. God has equipped us with His Holy Spirit to do that for us. We need only listen and obey—to be willing vessels for God to use in reaching our unbelieving loved ones. And I mean inspiration in the sense that we are encouraged by knowing that God can use us in such a noble fashion. He doesn't need to; He chooses to. He could do this all on His own, but He's selected each of us to be a letter of Christ to our unbelieving spouses right here and now.

So I ask you, what is your message to your unbelieving husband? What can you communicate through your actions today? Are you willing to let the Holy Spirit make His mark on you for the benefit of your husband?

Sacrificial Giving (Ouchies)

I will sacrifice a freewill offering to you;
I will praise your name, O Lord, for it is good.

PSALM 54:6

One Valentine's Day, I racked my brain about what to give my husband. I wanted to surprise him with something special, something out of the ordinary. Chocolates and a romantic card came to mind, of course, but I wanted something unique and longer lasting—maybe something that would even reflect the love God holds for him.

What could I give sacrificially to him to show how much I loved him? This line of thinking led me down a unique path. Instead of what I could do, I began thinking about what I should not do. So I made a list of four things I would not do, based upon areas that I saw needed improvement within myself.

1. No Nagging

Nagging has a really bad reputation, and for obvious reasons: It's ineffective and usually has the opposite of the desired effect. Plus, who wants to bear the title "nag"? I knew I didn't. So instead of getting frustrated when something I'd asked for was forgotten, I started making my husband a list. That way, I only had to remind him of the list and not each item.

In the past I'd resisted doing this because I thought him quite capable of doing it himself. But when he told me that the list helped him keep track of what needed to be done and that he preferred it, I quit resisting and made him one frequently. Instead of asking him to do something several times, I gently reminded him of the list. If it was one particular, important item or situation being neglected, I asked him if I could remind him again specifically of that item. When I asked for his permission first, he seemed much more receptive, which enabled me to hold the title of "helper" instead of "nag."

Now my husband is the one making his own lists. He caught on to the benefit and took control for himself. These days I simply ask him how his to-do list is going and will mention things for him to add to it. When I stopped nagging and found a solution that fit his needs, our conflict went away, and I didn't feel like his mother anymore. And I much prefer the title of helper.

2. No Expectations

I found that I usually had expectations when I made the self-centered assumption that my husband thought like I did. (Let me know when you've stopped laughing.) As I mentioned in chapter 4, I read several books on marriage. I also read books that would give me a male perspective. (*For Women Only* by Shaunti Feldhahn, *Surviving a Spiritual Mismatch in Marriage* by Lee and Leslie Strobel, and *What's He Really Thinking?* by Paula Rinehart are excellent resources.) I desperately wanted to better understand my husband's inner life and thought processes.

The more I read, the more I came to understand that many of my disappointments had come from expectations I'd placed upon him to fulfill needs he wasn't even aware of. Ladies, men truly can't read minds! (Color me surprised.) Instead of expecting him to understand what I needed or wanted and then winding up disappointed when he didn't come through, I learned (and still am learning) to simply tell him.

Amazingly, my husband had told me to do this before—many times in fact—but I hadn't taken him seriously. Why? Because I expected him to just get it, and I thought that explaining would take the romance out of our relationship. In the end, all I really accomplished was a heart full of resentment.

But in a spiritually mismatched marriage, this goes even deeper than just the usual and obvious differences between men and women. Whether your spouse follows another belief system or is simply agnostic or atheist, he will not comprehend the truth that you are following and believing, or even why. Christ invades our very being and replaces the lies with His truth. Thus, the mind and heart of a Christian operate on a different plane from that of an unbeliever. Just as we can't understand how our husband *can't* believe, he can't understand how we *can* believe.

Here's an example. Take the word "sin." Among Christians this word is often more familiar than we'd like to admit. I used to think of this word as being interchangeable with the word "wrong." One day, however, a discussion with my husband led to an interesting realization. Because my husband doesn't believe in God, he doesn't believe in sin. But he does distinguish right from wrong on a clear level, based on individual morality. To him "wrong" and "sin" aren't interchangeable. I'd made the false assumption that he thought as I did.

One of these days, I, like you, might just figure my man out, but only if it doesn't take the mystery out of the romance. In the meantime, it's important that we accept our husbands exactly where they are, appreciate our differences, and not expect them to make the same connections and understandings we do within a belief system he doesn't share. This is like expecting a child to walk at birth. It just won't happen until he learns to crawl first.

3. No False Assumptions

For some reason, our human nature seems to jump to the conclusion that when we are hurt or wronged, it's done intentionally. More often than not, I've found these wrongs stem from either miscommunication or misinterpretation, which lead to wrong assumptions. This is an area I have to work at very intentionally. I'm very good at putting the pieces together to form a conclusion that seems right, only to find out it's wrong. I learned this lesson the most effective way when someone—namely my husband—made a wrong assumption about why I said or did something. To be accused of something you didn't do or think is very hurtful.

Now I'm very careful to get my facts straight before I make any conclusions. This takes constant practice and awareness to retrain my nature so that my actions and reactions will follow suit. Again, here is an area where capturing our thoughts for Christ is not just inspirational but practical (see 2 Cor. 10:5).

4. No Resentment

It's easy to believe the patterns of the past and present will be the patterns of the future. This is definitely my weakness, but

I don't want to dredge up the past when a conflict arises and assume (there's that word again) that it will turn out the same. I want to believe the best outcome is possible.

Human nature doesn't make these situations any easier either. And the enemy uses them very strategically to attack our relationships and marriages. We fall into these vicious cycles of assumptions and resentments only to discover we are controlled by the ensuing chaos instead of being in control of our reactions, thoughts and beliefs. We become reactive instead of proactive.

So it boils down to this: Are we willing to move our own selfish wants and desires out of the middle of the equation and put our husband's in that place? To really put him first? Are we willing to sacrifice our selfishness and let the light of Christ shine through to this lost soul?

Let's just say I'm working on it. I'm a work in progress. We all are. We won't reach perfection by any means, but a willing heart is a good place to start. By living each day with the goal to be authentic—flaws and all—we have an opportunity to show our husbands how Christ is working in our own lives. (There's that present tense again.) Our perfection will not speak of Christ's presence in us, but our earnestness to overcome and be more Christlike will. That means we have to be willing to admit when we're wrong and to apologize—to allow our husband to see us intentionally working to overcome our faults, and to risk looking less than our best sometimes.

And the results? We'll leave those to God.

Discovery

Delving into some of these areas of authenticity can be challenging. Take a moment and pray, first asking the Holy Spirit to align your heart with God's. Tell Him you want to be willing to hear whatever He wants to tell you. Turning your will over to God, ready to submit to His guidance, is also an act of worship.

1. In what ways are you or can you be a fine "linen belt" in your marriage?

2. Are you authentic in your marriage? Are there areas, such as admitting you made a mistake, that are harder for you to be honest and transparent about?

3. Communication is vital to any marriage. In what ways do you and your husband struggle to communicate?

4. Is there a specific behavior or attitude you're willing to change for the sake of your marriage, even if you're the first and maybe the only one in the relationship making such a change? How can you show Christ to your spouse?

5. Think of something your spouse enjoys. How can you make a special effort to make it happen, as a surprise? Plan a date night, write a love letter, prepare a special meal, or just go for a walk. Be intentional about your time spent together, and then be consistent about it.

Prayer

Father God, You are so wise and perfect. I want to be that fine linen belt in my marriage. Please help me to let go of unrealistic expectations and seek You for what I need. Show me any areas where I've made false assumptions and

help me replace them with the truth. And, Lord,
reveal any resentment I'm still carrying around, so I may
repent and be free of a nagging attitude.

Lord, use me as Your parchment. Make me a love letter to
my husband. Show me how to show You, Jesus, our ultimate
love letter. Most importantly, Lord, show me how to be the
wife You need me to be for my husband. In Christ's most holy
and powerful name, amen.

Pick and Choose Your Battles

(Lynn)

*But make up your mind not to worry beforehand how
you will defend yourselves. For I will give you words and wisdom that
none of your adversaries will be able to resist or contradict.*

LUKE 21:14-15

It was December 25 and I was six years old. I don't remember
the events of this particular Christmas from my own memory,
but I share them with you as retold to me by my grandma. On
this particular Christmas, my mother was at the hospital deliv-
ering my baby brother. Yes, he was a Christmas baby, so was
my grandma and my son, a strange and interesting factoid
about our family.

Earlier in the morning, my parents had rushed out of the
house, leaving my younger sister and me at home with Grandma
and Papa. We adored our grandparents and, as was often the
case, my grandma sat down with me to play the board game
Marbles. Grandma placed the homemade wooden board on the
floor and counted out the different colored marbles and then
filled the spaces drilled to hold them. (Our version of Marbles resembles today's board game called Sorry.) Sitting opposite
Grandma, criss-cross applesauce, I squealed with excitement.

As a young child, I was clueless that my grandma was anxious over what was taking place at the hospital. I quickly scooped up the dice to start the game, oblivious to the tension etched on her face. I loved to play this game, and it's no wonder, because my grandma always let me win. (Grandmas are often like that.)

Grandma didn't pay too much attention to the play at hand. She was distracted, expecting the phone to ring any minute. As the clock ticked on, she grew increasingly uncomfortable sitting on the floor, pretending to listen to the latest trials and tales from Peruvian Park Elementary School's first-grade class. Grandma mindlessly clicked marbles across the board and tried to keep my young chatterbox energy from getting on her last nerve.

Finally, after an hour of my noise, the marbles clacking and still no word from Mom and Dad, she rolled the dice. In her haste to finish the game and call the hospital, Grandma rolled a six, clicked her last marble into the home spot, and said flatly to a tiny stunned face, "I won."

I bawled. I carried on. And I didn't stop.

As Grandma retold this story to me, we giggled at this silly moment of my childhood. She said to me, "You hated to lose, and I certainly learned that the hard way. I couldn't get you to stop crying for over an hour."

I hugged my grandma. She had me figured out at age six. However, it has taken a lifetime for me to admit that I hate to lose.

I have a competitive nature (but no more than the average woman) and over the years, I have learned to temper my competitive spirit. I have discerned under what circumstances it's best for me to give up or stand up. But when it comes to matters concerning my core values, I hate to give an inch of ground to anyone. I still don't like to lose.

Although this is a noble attribute in believers, it can create loads of conflict in a marriage.

Stand Up or Shut Up

Take a peek into a common point of contention in our home:

> The signature tune begins. The words "World News" appear on the television screen. I tense and mentally prepare myself for the battle soon to start. I spy my adversary from across the room. He glances suspiciously back at me, his eyebrow raised in a slight warning as he turns back to the screen. I continue with my covert observation as he leans toward the monitor.
>
> The lead story flashes the smiling picture of a controversial figure, a certain flash point between us. I cringe. World War III threatens to explode and shatter our carefully crafted peace. Artillery is readied and, sure enough, I open my big mouth and borders are crossed. A counter strike is inevitable.

Politics, religion and science are the usual issues that can launch the war of words around our house. *Why, oh, why don't I keep my big mouth shut?* Have you ever asked yourself this question a little too late?

Every marriage experiences conflict. However, disputes in a spiritually mismatched home are capable of elevating past a simple disagreement over something such as political preferences to a referendum on who each of us is as a person.

Let's think about this a minute. We believers view life through the lens of God's Word. We filter the day's events and process them through the truths we discover from our daily Bible reading and prayer time. Our husband processes life from some other source. We have two very different worldviews.

I admit this is a tough place to live. Especially when we begin to think about couples who are believers and who don't wrestle with differences in moral and faith issues. So we grapple with thoughts of either conquering (standing up) or surrendering (giving up). But today, let's be clear—it doesn't have to be one or the other.

Part of the process of becoming mature in Christ is learning to pick and choose one's battles carefully and prayerfully. Through godly wisdom, we are able to discern the unimportant issues as well as to remain steadfast to the principles for which the stakes are high. On certain points, then, we can simply agree to disagree with our husband.

For many years, I vehemently defended my every choice. My spouse and I would argue over the littlest of things, mainly because of my immaturity in Christ. I lived defeated because I took on the role of being Jesus. However, the truth is that Jesus doesn't need my defense. He is quite capable of defending Himself, thank you very much. He is God. Whew! What a relief.

Think about this Scripture:

Do not give dogs what is sacred; do not throw your pearls to pigs. If you do, they may trample them under their feet, and then turn and tear you to pieces (Matt. 7:6).

This passage is reflective of our situation. Unbelievers cannot comprehend many matters of faith by which we live our lives. When we try to share truth from the Bible, we are often given the eye roll or, worse, a criticism such as, "That's an old book, and it's irrelevant to today." Swine fail to appreciate the beauty of pearls; likewise, those who do not know the Holy Spirit cannot comprehend things of the Spirit. And, in most unequally yoked marriages, the more we push our faith on our husbands, the deeper they dig their heels in resistance.

The man without the Spirit does not accept the things that come from the Spirit of God, for they are foolishness to him, and he cannot understand them, because they are spiritually discerned (1 Cor. 2:14).

They just don't get it.

Using the bullhorn approach with our spouse reminds me of the uselessness of a resounding gong or a clanging cymbal referenced in 1 Corinthians 13:1. Loving our husband and living out our faith consistently, in a manner that reflects Christ's power of transformation, *is* possible. An unbelieving husband can't argue with the fact that he is living with an authentically changed wife. And that's the key: a transformed life.

Pick and choose battles that are of lasting importance. Stand up for principals, for they keep you from sinning. Stand on the authoritative truths laid out in God's Word.

Agree to disagree on the small stuff. Don't depend on your feelings for these choices, but look to guidance from the Bible, and pray, pray, pray. Consider the needs of others, yourself and your husband, and then decide if the issue at hand is truly worth conflict. Surrender your need to win. Let go of your desire to control. Be the peacemaker in your home, and let Christ handle the rest.

Jesus said, "Blessed are the peacemakers" (Matt. 5:9).

A Transformed Life

God is in the business of change. As long as we are breathing, He will be about the work of transforming our heart, character and soul. Our entire faith-walk is designed to conform us into Christ's likeness. Within our unequally yoked marriages, God's plan becomes remarkably apparent. The Lord will often employ conflict with our unbelieving spouse to bring about our transformation. Darn it!

For most of us, change can be frightening. It will shake our sense of security and stretch us in ways we are unprepared to handle, and sometimes we find adapting difficult. Therefore, we fight it. Add to this the fact that in most unequal relationships, the Lord always begins this change process with the woman. Darn it again!

Let me submit a thought for you to consider: In the Lord's eyes, we are highly prized to be in this very place. Through our heartaches, unfulfilled desires and soul-wrenching choices, we will burn away the dross to reveal a beautiful, refined woman—a woman after God's own heart.

Our husband's unbelief will lead us to the foot of the throne. We will understand the true power of prayer. We will be part of God's plan and purpose, and we will watch Him use us to influence the world around us. We will know love, joy, peace, patience, kindness and goodness, and our lives will honor Christ. Our conflicts at home will reshape us, teaching us to experience sacrificial and unconditional love. We will learn honest respect. We will overcome our fears, insecurity, selfishness, and superficial living. We will love our husband, our children and our neighbors with a full heart. More amazing still, we will love Jesus with all of our heart, soul, mind and strength.

Our fervent prayers will move heaven and earth to point our husband toward the cross of Christ. We are blessed and chosen as we walk this journey of the unequally yoked.

A transformed life is a thriving life.

Let's Have a Word

Conflict begins and ends with the words we speak. Did you know that our words have the power of life and death?

> The tongue can bring death or life; those who love to talk
> will reap the consequences (Prov. 18:21, *NLT*).

This proverb isn't a metaphor; it's truth. Think about the spoken word and how often it is used in the Bible. In the beginning, God said, "Let there be light" (Gen. 1:3). He spoke the universe into existence. John began his record of Jesus, "In the beginning was the Word, and the Word was with God, and the Word was God" (John 1:1). Jesus Himself emphasized the importance of what a person says:

> I tell you that men will have to give account on the day of judgment for *every careless word* they have spoken (Matt. 12:36, emphasis added).

The authority behind the words we speak to others or to ourselves cannot be overestimated. And when we speak words aloud into the spiritual realm, we unlock the power of God or we undo His carefully crafted plans:

> Reckless words pierce like a sword, but the tongue of the wise brings healing (Prov. 12:18).

The words that flow from our lips reflect the condition of our heart. Every day, we have the opportunity to bestow harm or healing. We can speak destruction into our relationships through gossip, sarcasm, cynicism, mockery and a host of other wicked and evil words. We can also speak words that bless others, such as, "I'm sorry," "I believe in you," "I am proud of you" and "I love you." It's a choice. Our words can bring healing to others and can precipitate tremendous healing in our own lives.

On the other side, we can steal back our prayers. For example, suppose we pray, asking the Lord's healing into our lives, claiming His promise in His Word. Then an hour later, we're on the phone, telling a friend that we feel as if we will never get better and how terrible we feel. This is like snatching your prayer right out of the air. This places the words of Matthew 21:22 into a whole new light: "If you believe, you will receive whatever you ask for in prayer."

I want the words I speak to be words that bring healing. How about you?

Speak Words of Grace

I remember a time in my marriage when I would try really, really hard to have an argument. I would launch into some discussion, trying to vent my anger. My husband, unwilling to respond and up the ante (in addition with his inability to get a word in edgewise), would ignore me, turn and walk away. This only infuriated me more. He would start down the hallway, seeking an escape as my harsh words barraged his ears. Did I let him go? Not a chance. I followed him with my resentment flying recklessly about our home and landing a direct hit on his spirit. Ouch.

Because I spent many years living in my stubborn refusal to agree to disagree, my husband and I argued frequently. And, ladies, females are much more clever and efficient with the verbal assault than men. We can fire off a round of blistering words faster than a woman can spot a bargain buy on the clearance rack. Our men can't keep up, and they go into retreat mode.

The area of words is where we need Christ the most. We need to practice, practice and practice managing the words we speak. Shouldn't the words we speak to our husbands be like the words we would speak to Christ, as we are His Bride? We need to voice words of encouragement. Words of support. Words of faithfulness, loyalty, friendship and honor.

A friend of mine who is living in her third decade of a spiritually mismatched marriage shared a simple sentence with me that caused me to change my words, and I will never forget it:

The words of his queen make him a king. It's the
building-up words spoken by a wife that make her
husband a better man. I don't ever want my hubby to
be built up by other women in the world—I want it to
be from me.

Such wise advice.

Let's determine to let our words bring healing and let
James 1:19 become our theme: "Be quick to listen, slow to
speak and slow to become angry." Then watch your husband
respond.

My husband and I still argue from time to time. After all,
we are human and our self-centered natures rise up and get in
the way. However, today my husband and I will often agree to
disagree. I am okay with this, because I turn it over to Jesus,
and I know His truth will prevail. I just keep praying that one
day my man will see from heaven's view.

Receive Grace

Speaking words of grace to our man is God's will for us as
wives. Likewise, the words we speak to ourselves are monu-
mentally important.

I was standing in the shower one morning and out of
nowhere, I began verbally beating myself up with condemning
self-talk. While shampooing my hair, thoughts of my distant
past came rushing forward. The ugliness and pain I had
caused others in the dark years of my prodigal detour hit me
like a ton of bricks: "How could *you do* such a thing? You deserve to die for the pain *you caused* your family. *You* are a really
bad person."

I could feel my spirit immediately sink into a familiar ditch.
I slunk from the shower, dressed and stood at the mirror to

brush my hair. As I worked at the snarls, it was as if the Holy Spirit arrived to smack me upside the head and say, "Don't you remember you were forgiven of these crimes long ago?"

I knew in that instant the enemy was up to his age-old tricks, speaking accusations meant to defeat my day and drag me away from the truth I have in Christ. What does God's Word say about our sins? They are as far away "as the east is from the west" (Ps. 103:12). That applies to me and to you. Period. The end.

When I hear the word "you" followed by an old and forgiven accusation, that's precisely when I take my thoughts captive to Christ and firmly reject the lies of the enemy. I am a new creation. I speak aloud the truth of this Scripture:

> Therefore, if anyone is in Christ, he is a new creation;
> the old has gone, the new has come! (2 Cor. 5:17).

As women, we can beat ourselves up with ugly self-talk. The harshest of words we often save to use upon ourselves. I am convinced that our negative self-talk is born out of our limited understanding and experience of God's perfect love. Perhaps when we were children our parents withheld love, or love was only given when we met certain conditions or expectations. Maybe someone we expected to always love us never did or rejected us. Perhaps right now we're not sure our husband loves us, or we have never felt as loved by our spouse as we expected to when we married. Possibly the very person who promised to love and protect us has betrayed us. Our experiences of love from human beings, who are imperfect and broken, taint the honest and pure love of Jesus Christ.

We cannot equate God's love for us by how we have been loved by others. God loves us with a vast, unending, protective affection. Read the following Scriptures out loud and ask the Lord to make them real, relevant and powerful in your heart:

The LORD himself goes before you and will be with you; he will never leave you nor forsake you. Do not be afraid; do not be discouraged (Deut. 31:8).

The king is enthralled by your beauty; honor him, for he is your lord (Ps. 45:11).

You have ravished my heart and given me courage, my sister, my [promised] bride; you have ravished my heart and given me courage with one look from your eyes, with one jewel of your necklace (Song of Sol. 4:9, *AMP*).

I [the Lord] have loved you with an everlasting love; I have drawn you with loving-kindness (Jer. 31:3).

And I pray that you, being rooted and established in love, may have power, together with all the saints, to grasp how wide and long and high and deep is the love of Christ, and to know this love that surpasses knowledge—that you may be filled to the measure of all the fullness of God (Eph. 3:17-19).

Jesus loves us to distraction. He will relentlessly pursue a love relationship with us forever. When we accept and live in the truth of the boundless love of Jesus, we become free to love others with authenticity.

Out of our hearts our words flow.

Discovery

You have the opportunity to bring about a practical change in your marriage relationship by choosing to change the words you use. Your spoken words can greatly impact your marriage, your children and the world around you. Take a minute to pray and ask the Lord about the words you speak. Would God approve of all of your words? Ask the Lord to help you make a real and lasting change in this area of your life.

1. What are several flash points that bring conflict in your marriage?

2. What would be a different approach to resolve conflict that would work for you in the future? Write out the words you will choose to use in the future to resolve conflict.

3. What was one time when you found yourself defending Christ to your unsaved husband? What was the result? Was this a stand-up or a shut-up moment? What would you do differently now?

4. What phrases can you choose to say to bless your spouse and children? Make a list of these words, and then make it a point this week to say them to your family.

5. What specifically can you do to be the peacemaker in your home?

6. Our God loves us so much that He will never leave us unchanged. What does this statement mean to you?

Select three of the Scripture verses from this chapter about the words we speak. Write them down on a small index card and carry them in your purse. Read them repeatedly. Once you memorize them, you will be astounded at how they will come to you in a time of conflict. You will discover how your responses change in the months ahead.

Prayer

Father, today I surrender my husband wholly to You. I am relinquishing my desire to save my husband, and I ask You to take Your rightful place in seeking and saving him for eternity. Lord, show me the areas of conflict I need to stand upon as well as issues I can surrender and trust You to handle. You tell us in Your Word that if we need wisdom, we should ask You for it and You will be generous in giving it to us [see Jas. 1:5]. Lord, place in my mind Your wisdom that I may be the peace-maker and the one to help resolve conflict with my spouse. Jesus, our words have the power of life and death, of cutting and healing. From this day forward, place a new awareness in my heart to be mindful of the words I speak to others. Place Your words in my conscious and unconscious mind so that only words that are good and pleasing come from my lips. Lord, "may the words of my mouth and the meditation of my heart be pleasing in Your sight" [Ps. 19:14]. In the powerful name of Jesus, amen.

Move from Hurt to Healing—
Seasons of Marriage
(Lynn)

Praise be to the God and Father of our Lord Jesus Christ,
the Father of compassion and the God of all comfort.

2 CORINTHIANS 1:3

A few years ago, my husband gave me a gift. Over the years, I have received many types of gifts from my man; however, this gift is the best one of all. He gave me a garden.

A garden is an unlikely present for a man to give a woman and even more peculiar when you consider that 10 years ago, if you had known me, you would have laughed yourself silly to think that Lynn Donovan would do anything domestic, let alone cultivate soil, risking dirt accumulating under her nails. It's true.

However, God in His amazing wisdom knew my soul craved more than working behind a desk, so He turned my world upside down, revealing something better. Isn't that just like Him? I left the corporate world of banking, and we moved out of state to a greener climate, leaving the desert behind. We settled into our new home and acclimated to our new surroundings. I discovered I enjoyed domestic life.

Several years passed before we decided to tear out our small backyard patch of grass and put in an area for a flower garden and boxes for vegetables. We hired Joe the Contractor, and within a couple of weeks he had recreated the yard to include roses, fruit trees, a birdbath, flowers and a perfect place to grow veggies. Every morning, weather permitting, I step out into the garden, sit down near the fire pit and sip hot coffee. There I talk with Jesus. I read my Bible, smell the flowers, and see the face of God in the beauty that surrounds me.

During the summer months, I walk through the garden, inspecting the rows of pepper plants and giant zucchini leaves, looking for any hints of new growth. I scour the tomato bushes on a seek-and-destroy mission, closely searching for those dreaded tomato hornworms. They give me the heebie-jeebies. Why God created them, I will never understand.

I pull the weeds and in July, I cook and preserve salsa like there is no tomorrow. Finally, in the fall, I pick the orange pumpkins to use in my fall decorating. The changes in my garden throughout the growing season are a delight to behold and a joy to my heart.

My garden is also a marker of sorts, a statement about the current season of my life. This season arrived after working through the planting process, pruning and weeding, and spreading the necessary but stinky fertilizer so that growth and, finally, veggies (or, better said, maturity) could occur. My garden is a reflection of my marriage journey.

Dineen and I often talk about the various seasons we have navigated through in marriage. It's interesting that each of us living in a spiritually mismatched marriage shares a commonality as we travel toward heaven. These seasons of the unequally yoked have unique characteristics and nuances.

Our early season begins long before our wedding day. As little girls, we play out our future in our imagination. We romanticize ourselves as the beauty, Cinderella, living happily ever after; and we know, without a doubt, that our Prince

Charming is out there, waiting to sweep us off our feet.

We marry and, indeed, life in the early years feels like Happily Ever After. In our haste to be pleasing to our groom, we are selfless and find it easy to let go of our personal preferences. As the months pass, however, we leave the loftiness of the honeymoon, reality settles in, our feelings are hurt, and our needs go unnoticed.

Surely if we just tell our prince what we need, he will be more than happy to oblige and fulfill our every longing.

"Sweetheart, let's go to church this Sunday. I sure have missed it."

"Church? You're kidding, right? You haven't gone to church since I met you."

This example may not be exactly how you first ventured into the spiritually mismatched camp, but it was likely something similar.

The early season of mismatchdom is filled with confusion and hurt compounded by a spiritual disconnect. We are either returning to our faith or have just become believers in Christ. Our spiritual muscle is tiny, and we flounder in this pool, some of us for a very long time. The pressure on our marriage escalates as children begin to arrive, and we struggle to manage the demands on our time and energy.

Slowly we move into the next season of our life. We grow in our faith, and the disconnect with our spouse intensifies. The more we learn about Jesus, the more we want to share Him with our husband. This season is a time of loneliness, more confusion, and struggling to understand the truth about our marriage. Grappling with the implications of this period is intense. We react and apply pressure on our spouse, fearing what may result if we arrive at an impasse.

We compound our fears with worry, as this is also the season in which our children are forming their faith. We spend hours agonizing over their spiritual upbringing. Add to this already tense situation the increasing pressure of managing a career, soccer games, ballet and every other activity imaginable. This season of marriage is where some of us can barely keep our heads above water. The enemy waits for this time in a marriage relationship so that he can work every opportunity to destroy what God will bless. This is the season where we discover the power of Christ in our midst. We wouldn't survive this season without Jesus.

Pushing past the loneliness, we discover our Prince, Jesus Christ, was always with us every step of the way. We grow in maturity through transformation cultivated through God's pruning and reshaping of us. The fruit from the years of reading God's Word and praying is beginning to reveal its power in our life, our kids and even our spouse. This season is worth the wait, worth the struggle, worth the day-by-day effort. That's a promise. But getting to the Promised Land means we must travel the road of forgiveness.

Travel the Road of Forgiveness

And do not grieve the Holy Spirit of God, with whom you were sealed for the day of redemption. Get rid of all bitterness, rage and anger, brawling and slander, along with every form of malice. Be kind and compassionate to one another, forgiving each other, just as in Christ God forgave you.
EPHESIANS 4:30-32

In the early years of my marriage, my husband held an atheistic worldview. He was convinced the Bible was a flawed book and irrelevant to our civilized culture today. I can't begin to count the number of verbal engagements in our home over this particular subject. Our disagreement over my beliefs regarding God's Word would flare up and sharp words would be exchanged. For me, these arguments brought with them a lot of pain.

The hurt I felt during this season of my life was real and could level me for several days. I literally felt pain in my chest, wounded by words spoken against Jesus, words spoken by my husband, my best friend on earth.

Part of my pain was due to my underdeveloped faith. It was difficult to cast off my husband's criticisms and rest in what I knew as truth. He was also good with scientific and intellectual comebacks. I was not. However, I look back on this period and can see it as a time when I grew very close to Jesus. In my pain, I would retreat to a quiet room and pray. Faithfully, Jesus would arrive, and I would feel Him wrap His arms around me and comfort me as He wiped away my tears.

I would step back into our marriage, assured that my faith remained intact. Yet there was a growing anger just under the surface of our relationship. My list of unmet needs was long. I regularly reviewed this growing list, ticking off each and every entitlement of married life that were mine but being withheld. Bitterness was born, birthed from an unforgiving heart.

This was another rubber-meets-the-road instance where I had to start doing the hard work that Jesus commanded. Do you remember the response Jesus gave Peter when he asked about forgiveness? I quoted part of this passage in chapter 2, but let's look at the entire story:

Peter came to Jesus and asked, "Lord, how many times shall I forgive my brother when he sins against me? Up to seven times?"

Jesus answered, "I tell you, not seven times, but seventy-seven times."

"Therefore, The kingdom of heaven is like a king who wanted to settle accounts with his servants. As he began the settlement, a man who owed him ten thousand talents [several million dollars in today's currency] was brought to him. Since he was not able to pay, the master ordered that he and his wife and his children and all that he had be sold to repay the debt.

"The servant fell on his knees before him. 'Be patient with me,' he begged, 'and I will pay back everything.' The servant's master took pity on him, canceled the debt and let him go.

"But when that servant went out, he found one of his fellow servants who owed him a hundred denarii [a few dollars in today's currency]. He grabbed him and began to choke him. 'Pay back what you owe me!' he demanded.

"His fellow servant fell to his knees and begged him, 'Be patient with me, and I will pay you back.'

"But he refused. Instead, he went off and had the man thrown into prison until he could pay the debt. When the other servants saw what had happened, they were greatly distressed and went and told their master everything that had happened.

"Then the master called the servant in. 'You wicked servant,' he said, 'I canceled all that debt of yours because you begged me to. Shouldn't you have had mercy on your fellow servant just as I had on you?' In anger his master turned him over to the jailers to be tortured, until he should pay back all he owed.

"This is how my heavenly Father will treat each of you unless you forgive your brother from your heart" (Matt. 18:21-35).

We forgive, because God forgives us.

Honest forgiveness isn't easy. In fact, it's hard—*very* hard. However, the Lord greatly desires to bring about healing in our lives. Scripture is full of passages of healing of the physical body as well as healing of the emotional injuries to the soul. Jesus' healing ministry was an integral part of His message in biblical times, and He is just as passionate about healing today.

If you remember, I shared with you about a time in my life when I was so angry with my husband that I refused to participate in a Bible study that might have required me to pray for his welfare. I was chock-full of resentment, and I felt justified in wearing my badge of bitterness on my shoulder. My legitimate needs were going unmet and when compared to other women in marriage, I felt I had been cheated out of all that marriage was supposed to be.

Comparing other marriages to my own is a toxic occupation. I coupled that with my growing unforgivenss, and I slipped off the path of thriving and into an unhappy life. Living on Unhappy Street is in direct contrast to what the Lord wants for us. I needed rescue from my resentment. But how? My anger was justified.

I began to pray, "Lord, help me to want to forgive."

Forgiveness doesn't mean forgetting all that transpired or minimizing the offense, nor is it given only if the offender is sorry. You aren't required to allow him or her to hurt you the same way again, and you can learn to institute healthy boundaries. In some situations outside of marriage, forgiveness doesn't even mean reestablishing friendship. However, forgiveness, especially within marriage, means relinquishing your right to get even and releasing your bitterness and resentment into the hands of Christ.

My friend Marian shared with me an exercise she uses to pray through forgiveness and to overcome the rawness of emotions:

· Admit the hurt and recognize that unforgiveness prevents living in the flow of God's love.
· Acknowledge the need for God's help as I choose to forgive.

- Imagine myself putting that situation, hurt or experience in the hands of Jesus.
- Ask God which good gift He gives me is to replace the pain and unforgiveness.
- Listen for His answer.
- Imagine myself embracing the gift He gave me in that moment, walking away, leaving the pain behind.

Through the transforming power of the Holy Spirit, we are able to do the hard work of forgiveness. And do you know what the result is? Freedom. The freedom to love our husband and the ability to trust the Lord for our marriage. We are freed of the hurts of unmet expectations. Jesus Christ is all about freedom. I didn't realize the darkness of my imprisonment until the day I forgave my husband's shortcomings and chose to love him for who he is. Isn't that what we want from our spouse? Isn't that what Christ gives us?

> He has sent me to bind up the brokenhearted, to proclaim freedom for the captives and release from darkness for the prisoners (Isa. 61:1).

I've lived many seasons unequally yoked and only now am I reaping the rewards of the hard work of forgiveness. I am able to teach my children about Christ, to love my husband unconditionally and to dwell daily in the presence of my Savior. But, because I have traveled through the difficult seasons where many of you are right now, I have a heart for your pain and I understand the real struggles you face. I have lived where you are living, and I wasted too many years stuck on the path. More than anything, I don't want one more woman wasting years imprisoned in a bad season. It is God's desire for us to discover that marriage is fun, fulfilling, rewarding and godly.

Godly? you may wonder. How can a believer and an unbeliever have a godly marriage?

For the rest of you who are in mixed marriages—Christian married to non-Christian—we have no explicit command from the Master. So this is what you must do. If you are a man with a wife who is not a believer but who still wants to live with you, hold on to her. If you are a woman with a husband who is not a believer but he wants to live with you, hold on to him. The unbelieving husband shares to an extent in the holiness of his wife, and the unbelieving wife is likewise touched by the holiness of her husband. Otherwise, your children would be left out; as it is, they also are included in the spiritual purposes of God (1 Cor. 7:12-14, *THE MESSAGE*).

Let this passage bring you comfort and security. You are a follower of Jesus, and it's by your faith that He will bring about His good and perfect will in your home. Can I get an amen? *Amen!*

A Front-Row Seat

The Lord willing, my husband and I have many more seasons ahead together. Recently we began sharing reading glasses at restaurants to see the menu. We giggle over the fact that our body parts don't work quite the same as in our early years, nor do they curve in the same places as when we were younger. But we don't care. It comes with the season.

In several years, my husband and I will face an empty nest and then, the Lord willing, the delightful season of grandchildren will arrive. Finally, we will grow old together. As I am writing this, I have a lump in my throat. Time passes quickly.

I am excited to take each step, holding the hand of my husband and the hand of Jesus. Adventure and laughter await. We have each other, and our marriage is blessed with intimacy, trust, transparency, adoration, friendship and the love of God.

Our happy marriage is possible because Jesus stepped into the life of an ordinary woman. I have full confidence that the Lord is working out all things for His honor and glory to culminate on the day my husband crosses over the line and into God's kingdom. While I wait, I do my part. I love. I trust. I pray. I live for Christ.

Living in a crazy, mixed-up, uniquely yoked marriage has its astounding moments. I discovered I have a front-row seat to the grandest drama ever told: The supernatural salvation story of an ordinary man as it plays out before my eyes. Jesus thrills my heart with the outrageous and miraculous as He pursues my husband with a relentless vigor and through unexpected experiences.

Do you remember that I mentioned Joe the Contractor? He saw my vision for the garden and made it come to life. He dug up the grass and shrubs, laid down sprinkler lines and poured cement. He worked in our backyard for only two short weeks, yet I will never forget him.

Two days into our garden project, it was obvious that Joe was a Christian. Each morning when he arrived, he plugged his radio into an outside outlet and blasted Christian music for all the neighbors to enjoy—whether they wanted to hear it or not. Each evening as Joe got ready to leave, my husband and I would join him on the patio to talk about the work, family, or whatever else came to mind. We enjoyed Joe very much and, interestingly, he was never shy to share little tidbits of faith with my husband while he dusted the dirt from his pants and whacked the mud from his gloves.

Two weeks passed quickly. When the backyard project was complete and it was time for Joe to leave, my husband and I

met him out in front of the house to finish our business trans-
action, thank him for his hard work, and praise his workmanship. As we stood in the driveway, Joe told us a story about the
electrical contractor working on our project, whose name was
also Joe, and how he had led him to Christ that very day in
our backyard.

Joe said, "I led him in the sinner's prayer, and he was saved
today."

I was stunned and thrilled, "Joe, that's awesome."

I observed my husband's interest from the corner of my eye
as he listened. Joe quickly moved on with the conversation, now
turning and looking directly at my man.

"Are you saved?" Joe was blunt.

My husband shook his head.

I jumped in and stated, "He is a holdout." (Sometimes I
should just keep my mouth shut.)

Joe pushed on, his face to my husband's face.

"I was once just like you. I didn't believe. I was a self-reliant
man. I didn't need the Lord. My life was good without Him."
Without hesitation or invitation, Joe shared his salvation experience, his eyes locked with my husband's as he spoke each word.

I stared in disbelief as the scene unfolded before me, barely
able to take it all in.

"My wife made me go with her to a Carmen concert," Joe
said. "As I sat in the chair at the end of the concert, the altar
call was made. I saw hundreds of people going forward. I was
curious. *What do these people know that I don't know?* I had to
know, so I stood up and went down to the floor to find out.
That night I prayed to receive Christ.

"However, after the prayer I felt nothing. It wasn't until the
next day that the Lord took hold of me and began to change
my life. That very day God stirred up a strong desire in me to
read the Bible. So I did."

Joe added, "It was my wife's prayers for me over the years that made a difference."

I was stunned to silence, a rare event indeed, and I watched as my husband absorbed Joe's story. Mind you, we were smack in the middle of our driveway in front of the neighbors.

Joe looked intently into my man's face and said, "I was just like you."

He paused, his eyes remaining firmly fixed upon my husband.

Then Joe asked, "Do you want to pray with me?"

I couldn't believe this was happening right in front of my eyes. My husband looked at Joe and said, "*Yes.*"

Joe reached out with both hands and said, "Give me your hands." They joined hands. "Repeat after me." Then Joe led my husband through the prayer of salvation. I heard my husband ask for forgiveness and acknowledge Jesus as Lord.

It happened.

Right there.

On the driveway.

Two men holding hands in broad daylight.

Now that's what I call a front-row seat!

The follow-up to this story isn't what you might expect. My husband told me the next day that he had been taken off guard by Joe and wasn't really sure he was ready to make a decision of faith.

I was disappointed but thrilled at the same time. Jesus displayed His purpose through these events and still today, I am blown away to consider the lengths my God will go to reach one man for eternity.

Trust in the LORD with all your heart and lean not on your own understanding (Prov. 3:5).

We cannot fathom why we must live through the difficult seasons of our mismatched marriage. We can't begin to understand the details of God's doings, and we grow discouraged when we don't get answers to the whys of our hurts. We don't comprehend God's plans for us or our spouse, but once in a great while, He allows us a glimpse of the miraculous. That's more than enough for me.

Our Lord loves my husband (and yours) more than I can even imagine. I am convinced, without a doubt, that Jesus has a multitude of encounters lined up and waiting in my husband's future, just like the one he had with Joe. And I have a front-row seat to watch the astonishing unfold. So pull up a chair, my friends. We are on one crazy, challenging but fantastic journey. The best is yet to come, and it's all because of Jesus.

Discovery

Whatever your current season of marriage, the Lord is beside you. You can believe that He is working for the good of those who love Him, who have been called according to His purpose. Pray and ask the Lord to reveal His purposes for you, your marriage and your future together. Ask Him to uncover areas of unforgiveness and place them at the foot of the cross. He has an amazing adventure for us and will bring our husband along in His perfect timing.

1. What is the current season of your marriage? *Empty nest and grandchildren*

2. What are the expectations and entitlements that remain unfulfilled in your marriage? Examine your list. Determine to see them in the light of God's purpose. Begin to pray this week that the Lord will help you release any bitterness you have in your heart. Write a quick prayer right now. *Jesus,*

3. Look up Psalm 139:23-24. How does this Scripture apply to your marriage? *hurt, bitterness, be patience w/ Jesus timeline*

* Psalm *

4. In this chapter, my friend Marian shares the way
she prays through forgiveness. What is one area of
unforgiveness that you will work through using
this process? Write down the date and a commitment to Christ to see this process through to its
conclusion. *Tom's words when she is angry & tired*

5. Can you remember a time you had a front-row seat
to watch something God was doing? Describe what
happened. *none ... god ...*

6. What is God's calling for your future?
God search my thoughts to reveal sin to live "the path of everlasting life

Prayer

*Jesus, from this day forward, change my heart to see the
miraculous around me. Help me to release the expectations and
entitlements I have held tightly in my grip and rejoice in the
things I have that are of lasting importance, such as my husband,
my children, my family and the kingdom of God. Lord, reveal
the areas of unforgiveness that are holding me hostage to pain.
I release them to You and ask that You place a balm of healing
over those scars. Father, when I am hurt in the future,
be my protector and give me the grace to release all bitterness
before it gets stored in my heart. Jesus, I long to sit in the front
row and watch You perform miracles in the life of my husband.*

*Let me be a prayerful participant, and I thank You now
for the work You are already doing to bring about my spouse's
salvation. Jesus, You are the reason I live and breathe. I praise
You. I worship You. I will live my life for You. In Your
name I pray all these things, amen.*

Keep Your Armor On—
You're at War!

(Dineen)

Finally, be strong in the Lord and in his mighty power. Put on the full armor of God so that you can take your stand against the devil's schemes. For our struggle is not against flesh and blood, but against the rulers, against the authorities, against the powers of this dark world and against the spiritual forces of evil in the heavenly realms.

EPHESIANS 6:10-12

The Battle We Can't See

If you are like me, you most likely get pulled in multiple directions on a daily basis. Interruptions abound, and your self-identity is as apparent and flittering as the steam on the bathroom mirror. That's if you even got a shower today. You're a mother, a wife, an administrative assistant, a maid, a butcher, a baker and a candlestick maker. Your job changes according to what time of day it is.

So often our lives become more about what's going wrong than what's going right. How can it not when we are barraged moment to moment by the same circumstances or new ones compounding the old? By the end of the day, our brains feel like a battlefield and our hearts have the holes to show the direct hits we've taken.

We wonder how much longer we can continue. What would happen if we just stopped? Or maybe we stand somewhere, staring off into space, having one of those "Christmas Story" daydreams where our family falls weeping at our feet when they realize that our current death sentence is due to their lack of help, understanding and appreciation. I did this very thing as I emptied the dryer late one night.

During this briefest of pity parties, I realized it was time to step back, retreat and find shelter in the only One who can bring relief to war-weary hearts and restore strength for the next battle. And to do all this, I needed armor:

> For our struggle is not against flesh and blood, but against the rulers, against the authorities, against the powers of this dark world and against the spiritual forces of evil in the heavenly realms. Therefore put on the full armor of God, so that when the day of evil comes, you may be able to stand your ground, and after you have done everything, to stand. Stand firm then, with the belt of truth buckled around your waist, with the breastplate of righteousness in place, and with your feet fitted with the readiness that comes from the gospel of peace. In addition to all this, take up the shield of faith, with which you can extinguish all the flaming arrows of the evil one. Take the helmet of salvation and the sword of the Spirit, which is the word of God (Eph. 6:12-17).

There are actually two parts to this Scripture passage. The first part is verse 12, which talks about what or whom we're battling. It's hard to fight something we can't outright see. If you swing a baseball bat at me, I'm going to duck. If you insult me, I'm going to get mad. But how do we battle an enemy we can't see, touch or even kick? (Now there's a great mental image: "Come here, Satan, and meet my foot.")

The second part is the standing part, described in verses 13-17. These verses don't tell us to don our armor and rush into battle. They don't tell us to slash wildly and leave a wake of destruction. No, they tell us to stand firm. In fact, the word "stand" is used three times and in close proximity. Why?

I did some searching, and I found out that *histemi*, the original Greek word translated as "stand" in this passage, is an active verb. In this context, it means to stop, stand still, stand immovable, stand firm, continue safe and sound, stand unharmed, stand ready or prepared.

God is our commander. He is the one who is directing the battle, our lives, everything. If we're racing into battle with only the sound of our raging voices in our ears, how on earth will we be able to hear Him tell us when to strike and when to fall back?

God has the big picture. He knows the lay of the land. He's the One who will get us through the war alive. And kicking, I might add.

Of all the calls to the Christian life, I think this is the most challenging. It falls into that faith-and-trusting area. We have to trust that God is there, and we have to believe that the battle is all around us. We can walk blindly through and let the repercussions knock us off our feet, or we can go into battle prepared with armor.

Believe it or not, we're on the front lines in our mismatched marriage. When there's a soul at stake, the enemy will do everything he can to keep that person from coming to Christ. Fortunately for us, Satan doesn't know the big picture, nor can he usurp God's plan for our loved one. He can, however, try to tear us down and destroy our testimony. That's why it's so important to wear our armor daily.

The Belt of Truth

Jesus answered, "I am the way and the truth and the life.
No one comes to the Father except through me."

JOHN 14:6

In the Bible, Jesus always told the truth (all four Gospel writers record many instances of Jesus prefacing His remarks by saying, "I tell you the truth"), and He even referred to Himself as the truth (see John 14:6 above). The belt in our armor symbolizes our relationship with Christ and is firmly set in truth. The enemy will slam us repeatedly with lies to make us doubt, question and despair. We need this belt to discern the truth, so don't bury it. Wear it proudly buckled around your waist and remember that with it, you are eternally bound to Christ, no matter what happens. His love is not dependent upon anything, isn't conditional and won't deteriorate over time.

The Breastplate of Righteousness

It is because of him that you are in Christ Jesus, who has become for us
wisdom from God—that is, our righteousness, holiness and redemption.

1 CORINTHIANS 1:30

Our righteousness comes from Christ, pure and simple. When God looks at us, that's what He sees: the righteousness of His Son. Beneath this breastplate is our heart. There sits our emotions, our self-worth and our trust. Without this coverage, we are vulnerable in the most basic of ways. The enemy will skew our feelings toward our spouse, leaving fertile soil ripe for planting seeds of resentment, misunderstanding and judgment. He will make us feel less than adequate to please our spouse, and he will undermine our trust in God as well as in our husband.

Attacking relationships is a finely honed skill of the enemy. This breastplate, handcrafted by the blood of Christ Himself, is the barrier to protect us from the enemy's attempts to discourage and defeat us.

The Shoes of the Gospel of Peace

The rain came down, the streams rose, and the winds
blew and beat against that house; yet it did not fall, because
it had its foundation on the rock.

MATTHEW 7:25

Our footgear is the Word of God and the good news of Jesus, but in order to be ready to share our faith, we need to be securely grounded. Time spent in God's Word, learning about Him and coming to know His character, is vital to this process. As unequally yoked spouses, we're more likely to share our faith through actions instead of words. So I tend to take this literally. We have to be ready to move into action when God calls us. With Jesus as our foundation, we can run the race with feet fitted in the finest footgear there is—God's Word.

The Shield of Faith

Let us fix our eyes on Jesus, the author and perfecter of our faith,
who for the joy set before him endured the cross, scorning its shame,
and sat down at the right hand of the throne of God.

HEBREWS 12:2

Personally, I consider the shield of faith our most important piece of armor. A strong faith can protect us from so much. And just like a piece of real armor, our faith needs care and constant upkeep. According to Hebrews 12:2, Jesus is not only the perfecter of our faith but also the author of it as well. Understanding this verse released me from the burden of thinking it was my job to have enough faith. But just like the father whose demon-possessed son was healed by Jesus, we too can say, "I do believe; help me overcome my unbelief!" (Mark 9:24). We too can ask God to help us believe and strengthen our faith, especially during those times when praying for our spouse seems hopeless or even pointless.

The true strength of our faith lies in God, not our circumstances. So let's consider a difficult question: Can we love our spouse without any guarantee that he will come to know Christ? If this question raises despair, then we've most likely placed our faith in our spouse's conversion and not in God. This is a key element to thriving in our mismatched marriage. Realigning our faith to reside completely in God can be difficult, but it is absolutely necessary to finding peace and to loving our spouse unconditionally. Leave the saving to Jesus. You do the loving!

Ultimately, this is what our faith journey is truly about—not only growing in faith and trust but also placing our faith in our most capable and wonderful God. Then we are protected by His strength and not our own. Now that's a shield that won't rust or fail!

The Helmet of Salvation

Do not conform any longer to the pattern of this world, but be transformed by the renewing of your mind. Then you will be able to test and approve what God's will is—his good, pleasing and perfect will.
ROMANS 12:2

The enemy loves to attack our thoughts and inject his lies, especially when it comes to our salvation. He can't snatch eternity away from us, but he can plant just enough doubt to make us ineffective Christians. That's his goal: to take away our testimony and keep us from being an example of Christ to our spouse. The helmet of salvation is our protection against these doubts and lies.

The Sword of the Spirit

*We demolish arguments and every pretension that sets itself
up against the knowledge of God, and we take captive every
thought to make it obedient to Christ.*

2 CORINTHIANS 10:5

Of all our pieces of armor, the sword of the Spirit is our only weapon of offense. The other pieces defend and protect us, but we need the sword to fight. This sword is the Word of God. If we don't spend time reading the Bible and studying God's Word, we are ill equipped to oppose the lies of the enemy with truth. Our sword is vital to protect our marriage. The Bible is our greatest weapon. Nothing can stand against God's Word, which is His truth and also His Son (see John 1:14).

We absolutely must wear our armor at all times. Don it every day. Literally pray through these verses from Ephesians and imagine yourself putting each piece of armor into place. That's basically what quiet time spent each morning with God is all about: to regroup, to re-armor and to know God's heart and praise Him for another day, prepared to fight and win.

And don't forget your silver polish.

Don't Be a Martyr, Be a Missionary

*But the Lord is faithful, and he will strengthen and protect
you from the evil one.*

2 THESSALONIANS 3:3

As we walk through life, we collect labels of different sorts. "Mother," "wife," "assistant," "doctor," "teacher"—these are rather innocuous labels that simply explain a role. Then there are descriptive labels that build us up ("beautiful," "talented," "graceful") or tear us down ("ugly," "stupid," "clumsy"). Finally, there are the labels that describe our marital situation—"divorced," "widowed," "spiritually mismatched."

The interesting thing about any kind of label is that it can be just a word we barely notice or a heavy burden that weighs us down in every area of our lives. We walk around wearing these signs as if they were a punishment or a jail sentence.

As the believing spouse in a mismatched marriage, we have to be careful not to wear our label of "unequally yoked" like a martyr. The danger of such an outlook is that our perceived label implies that our husband is our burden. Don't think your man doesn't pick up on this. He does. He knows full well how he's reflected in your eyes.

The key is to change our perceptions and quit seeing ourselves as martyrs in our marriages. Instead, we need to put on the label of missionaries. As I said in chapter 5, we are the aroma of Christ in our homes, to our husband and to our family. If we only see our man as a burden to be dealt with instead of the husband God is calling us to love unconditionally, I can guarantee that's not perfume we're wearing.

We need to think of ourselves as soldiers on the front lines of our marriage. Our husbands need us fully armored at all times, even if they are completely unaware of the battle raging around them. We have the opportunity to be the catalyst of prayer, unleashing God's power and protection in their lives.

God has placed us where we are for such a time as this (like Esther), and we must be prepared. He has entrusted us with the label of "unequally yoked" for a noble cause: (1) to be the closest representation of Christ in the life of our husband, and (2) to be a soldier on the front line to battle for our husband's soul. You never know when your husband might start asking you questions, and you must always be aware that he's watching your actions closest of all. Do your actions line up with your words? Do they outweigh your words? Do they affirm your words? As mentioned previously, our actions will always speak louder than anything we say.

One day as I was driving to meet my husband for lunch, I sensed a sudden urgency to pray for him. As I did, an image of him surrounded by flashes of light and dark filled my mind. I knew in that moment that a battle raged around my husband, and God had called me to don my armor and join the fray with my prayers. Scriptures came to mind in rapid fire as I prayed for my husband's protection and salvation.

We don't know what battles are waging around our unbelieving spouse, but God's Word is clear about our true struggles being in the spiritual realm. To this day, I still don't know what the battle surrounding my husband was all about, but I was so grateful for the time I'd spent studying God's Word. An unopened Bible is like sending a soldier into battle without protective gear and weapons. Without such gear, the soldier is vulnerable and ineffective. God gave us His sword—His Word—to wield, not to collect dust.

Keep in mind too that no soldier stands alone. He or she is part of a larger force that supports him or her and is ready to jump into battle when needed. Nor can we, as unequally yoked wives, stand alone in this gap for our husbands or for ourselves. The prayers of others are vital, not only for our spouse's salvation but also for our own perseverance and protection. Pray and ask God to put key people in your life who, like fellow soldiers, can be trusted with your prayer needs and are committed to praying for you and your husband.

No soldier stands alone—nor can a spiritually mismatched wife.

Basic Training

But even if you should suffer for what is right, you are blessed.
"Do not fear what they fear; do not be frightened." But in your hearts set
apart Christ as Lord. Always be prepared to give an answer to everyone
who asks you to give the reason for the hope that you have. But do this
with gentleness and respect, keeping a clear conscience, so that those who
speak maliciously against your good behavior in
Christ may be ashamed of their slander.

1 PETER 3:14-16

As I shared in my story at the beginning of this book, not long after I'd recommitted my life to Christ, my husband decided he was an atheist. This didn't mean he was no longer interested in my faith. Quite the opposite, in fact.

He would periodically ask me questions in regard to the Bible or my beliefs. Because of my insecurity about saying the wrong thing, coupled with a limited knowledge of the Bible, my answers often sounded incomplete and ungrounded, even to my own ears. Finally, one day when I was confused and frustrated by what I perceived to be an interrogation, I asked my husband why he asked me so many questions. He said he wanted to be sure that my faith choice was what I truly believed and not something I was just being fed and led around like a mindless follower.

From that day on I determined that I had to know that what I believed was based on what the Bible said, not just on the pastor's Sunday sermon or something a friend shared with me. I needed to study the Bible daily, attend Bible studies and research areas in which I was unsure. I am most grateful for a mentor who came alongside me during this time and wisely nudged me to a daily quiet time of Bible study and prayer. Her years of intimacy with God gave her amazing wisdom.

A couple years ago, my husband started asking more questions about the Bible due to the particularly hot climate present in California politics. I found myself being asked questions about the Bible and my beliefs that ran me in circles.

Why? Because, like water running down a funnel to a final destination, the ultimate answer never failed to wind up at the cross of Christ. I had to give the reason behind my hope. The frustrating part was that no matter how I tried to explain myself, my answers didn't seem to satisfy him.

One night after two hours of this dance of endless loops into the wee hours of the night, I said, "Enough." I was exhausted. He left the room and I wept, feeling like a complete failure. Why had my answers fallen on such unreceptive ears? Why hadn't God arrived and brought the salvation message home to my husband's heart?

As I cried and prayed, God's soft voice crept in and told me that I'd done exactly as He had asked me to. I'd given the reason behind my hope. I'd shared His Son. Then He said to leave the rest to Him. Though I hadn't witnessed a dramatic conversion in my husband, God affirmed my actions of being faithful to share what I knew.

We never know when we'll be called into action, but in the meantime, we have the chance to prepare for battle. God's Word is our most valuable weapon against the enemy who is bent on keeping our husbands from coming to know Christ and determined to destroy our marriages.

As wives, we have the opportunity to be proactive with our prayers in the lives of our husbands, with whom we can't vocally share our faith and the Bible. We may not be able to win our husband's salvation with our words, but our prayers are the substance of miracles.

Discovery

Before you begin the study questions, ask God to show you any areas of your marriage that are vulnerable and to lead you to Scriptures to pray for your spouse and for your marriage and family.

1. In what areas of your life and your marriage has the enemy gained a foothold? *Helmet of Salvation Sword of the Spirit*

2. In what ways do you (or can you) show your faith to your spouse without using any words? *tell Tom I love him and respect Tom Forgive Tom*

3. Is your faith (your obedience to God, your peace, your trust) dependent upon your spouse's salvation? Why or why not? *no Jesus will Christ is responsible for his salvation*

4. What piece of your spiritual armor needs the most polishing? *The Shield of Faith*

5. Do you have a special time set aside each day to spend with God alone—to pray, to worship, to study His Word and to equip yourself? If not, make a commitment now to spend 10 or 15 minutes with God at the start of your day. Set aside a special spot and keep your Bible and study materials there (if you can). Then keep that appointment every day for a month. You'll be surprised at how that 10 or 15 minutes winds up being 20 or 30 minutes or even longer.

6. Think of two or three people who you would feel comfortable approaching for prayer. Make a commitment to contact them this week and ask them to be part of a prayer team for you and your husband. *Marilyn Rylander and Barb Young*

Prayer

Father God, I praise You and thank You for this armor
You have given me. Help me each day to don the helmet of
salvation to keep my thoughts secure in Your truth,

*the breastplate of righteousness to guard my heart,
the belt of truth to gird my life with Your truth, the shield of
faith to keep the enemy away, and the sword of the Spirit to
fight for my husband. Lord, You are the author and perfecter
of my faith. Keep me centered in You. Put a burning desire
and an unquenchable hunger in my heart for Your Word and
for time with You. Help me keep my armor shiny so that I
may see Your reflection in every inch of it. In Christ's most
holy and strong name, amen.*

Learn When to Pray the Most Dangerous Prayer

(Dineen)

You will keep in perfect peace him whose mind is steadfast,
because he trusts in you.

ISAIAH 26:3

John the Baptist

John the Baptist stayed on my mind heavily one week. I wondered what he might have felt if he had seen Jesus with the Twelve. Did he wish to be one of those men chosen to follow Jesus, constantly in the presence of the Son of God? Did he question why he'd been set apart? Or did he actually have the better job than those of the Twelve?

Even as an unborn baby, John seemed to know what his life was about and for. In utero, he "leaped for joy" at the sound of Mary's voice (Luke 1:44). Before he was even born, his path was set—what he would eat, how he would dress and what his mission would be. He was even filled with the Holy Spirit from birth.

But still . . . did he wonder, question or sometimes even desire to switch places with one of the disciples? Or was he completely at peace with his place in preparing the way for Jesus?

The next day John saw Jesus coming toward him and said, "Look, the Lamb of God, who takes away the sin of the world! This is the one I meant when I said, 'A man who comes after me has surpassed me because he was before me.' I myself did not know him, but the reason I came baptizing with water was that he might be revealed to Israel. . . ."

The next day John was there again with two of his disciples. When he saw Jesus passing by, he said, "Look, the Lamb of God!"

When the two disciples heard him say this, they followed Jesus. Turning around, Jesus saw them following and asked, "What do you want?"

They said, "Rabbi" (which means Teacher), "where are you staying?"

"Come," he replied, "and you will see."

So they went and saw where he was staying, and spent that day with him. It was about the tenth hour.

Andrew, Simon Peter's brother, was one of the two who heard what John had said and who had followed Jesus. The first thing Andrew did was to find his brother Simon and tell him, "We have found the Messiah" (that is, the Christ). And he brought him to Jesus.

Jesus looked at him and said, "You are Simon son of John. You will be called Cephas" (which, when translated, is Peter) (John 1:29-31,35-42).

What struck me about the above verses was how the two disciples following John left him to follow Jesus. One of them was Peter, the one whom Jesus planned to build His church upon. This episode again illustrates John's mission to prepare things for Jesus. He enlisted these two men for the Messiah's cause and then released them to the Lord he had faithfully served.

But again, did he wonder? Did he watch these men go with Jesus and long to go with them? Did he question why he wasn't destined to be one of the Twelve—a confidant and friend to the long awaited One? After all, he'd spent his whole life preparing for this time, hadn't he? At least as far as what we're told in the Bible, his life course was set from the womb. And as we know from God's Word, John's course was set even before that (see Ps. 139:13-16).

We could argue that John didn't wish or long to be a part of this select group because his calling was as necessary as that of Jesus' disciples. He had his place, his role to play in a most important story. But I can't help but think that some small and very human part of him wanted to be included, to be like Andrew and Peter, to fit into the elite group, instead of walking a seemingly lonely path to his death.

How often have we found ourselves in this very same position? Wishing we were someplace else. Comparing our place with that of others and longing for the same circumstances. Watching couples at church, and aching to know, even just for a moment, what it feels like to have our husband at our side worshiping the one true God. Longing to know what it's like to pray with him over the issues we're facing together. Desperate for our children to see us both united by a common faith.

Maybe John did feel left out, and maybe while he sat in prison he did wish he could have been one of the disciples instead of missing all the action. But he must have overcome those feelings and doubts because, even when it meant risking everything, he did what he had been sent to do. He spoke the truth and stayed his course.

The path of the unequally yoked is one of the hardest I've ever had to walk, and I'm still walking it. It's easy to get lost in wishes, wonderings and longings and miss the big picture. John may not have had the glory of the Twelve, but he proved himself faithful and never wavered in his service. He may have had doubts, but he didn't run away or give up.

Perhaps the answer is in his words: "He must become greater; I must become less" (John 3:30). Even when he sat in prison, John never doubted his role or the coming of the Messiah. Though he sent his men to confirm Jesus' identity, John never doubted that the true Messiah would come (see Matt. 11:2-3).

John's resolve and strength came from having the Holy Spirit. He wasn't sent on his mission and left to flounder, and we aren't either. Jesus sent reassurance to John, letting him know his cause was just and complete, and He praised John for the work he'd done (see Matt. 11:7-15).

In those glimpses we catch the real role of John. He didn't come to serve men but to serve Christ. In the end, it didn't matter how he fit in or what he did or didn't have. He fulfilled his calling to prepare the way for Jesus. As simple as that.

Truth be told, we are in a similar position. We are like John to our husbands, preparing for the day when Jesus lays claim on their lives. At times God reveals our mission only on a need-to-know basis, bit by bit. Other times, He gives us a sense of the critical role we play in our husband's lives B.C. (before Christ) and will play A.C. (after Christ).

One aspect is certain though: this is our mission. God has placed us here for this time and this reason, to be instrumental in our husband's salvation.

John kept his eyes on Jesus. He knew it wasn't about him but about the mighty God he served. And that's where we find inspiration. John's story wasn't about him; it was about Jesus. Just as our story isn't about us; it's about preparing the way for Jesus in the life of our husband.

Motivated by *Agape* Love

When they had finished eating, Jesus said to Simon Peter, "Simon son of John, do you truly love me more than these?"

"Yes, Lord," he said, "you know that I love you."
Jesus said, "Feed my lambs."
Again Jesus said, "Simon son of John, do you truly love me?"
He answered, "Yes, Lord, you know that I love you."
Jesus said, "Take care of my sheep."
The third time he said to him, "Simon son of John, do you love me?"
Peter was hurt because Jesus asked him the third time, "Do you love
me?" He said, "Lord, you know all things;
you know that I love you."

JOHN 21:15-17

After looking at John one day, I found my interest sparked by Peter. In John 18, Peter denied Christ three times. Then in John 21, Jesus asked if Peter loved him three times. I love the symbolism here, and again, God brings more than one purpose to light.

Just as Peter denied Christ three times, Jesus gave Peter the chance to choose Him three times, thereby reaffirming Peter's place in relationship to God's kingdom and also to Christ Himself. If we dig a little deeper, though, into the original Greek words, we find another layer of meaning, because two different Greek words are both translated as "love."

The first time Christ asked Peter, "Simon son of John, do you love me more than these?" He used the Greek word *agape*, which describes a love that is volitional (a choice) and self-sacrificing. Peter answered, "Yes, Lord, you know that I love you." But in this verse, he uses the Greek word *phileo*, which means a brotherly love with common interests.

The second time Christ asked Peter the same question, He again used the word *agape*. And again, Peter answered by using *phileo*. Finally, when Jesus asked Peter the same question for a third time, He too used *phileo*. In a sense He was asking Peter, "Are you really my friend?" Peter didn't quite seem to catch on to what Jesus was really asking him and, though hurt,

Peter affirmed his love for Christ, using the same word he had the previous two times: *phileo*.

I almost wonder if Peter was afraid to confess such devotion. Had he really had time to process the fact that the man he had once professed was the Messiah, then denied and watched crucified, had truly come back to life? He and the other disciples had gone from the mountaintop experience of being in the presence of the Son of God on a daily basis, to what they perceived as all their hopes broken just as Christ's body had been. Perhaps Peter struggled with his belief or, more importantly, was afraid to hope.

Phileo love is a relatively easy place to be. We can love someone who likes the same things we do, thinks the same way we do and especially shares the same beliefs we do. But in an unequally yoked marriage, this form of love doesn't work for long. (And I believe this is true for marriage in general.) We aren't in such a mutual relationship. Our spouse doesn't share our same beliefs and thus the grounds for the *phileo* form of love can turn into bitter resentment.

So Christ calls us to an *agape* form of love—a love based upon a decision, not a feeling; a love that is self-sacrificing, not self-serving.

Which form of love we profess is determined by our motivation. *Phileo* love implies affiliation for mutual benefit. *Agape* love is a commitment without expectation of anything in return. We're either smack dab in the middle of it, looking to satisfy our own needs through mutual affiliation, or we're not even looking to ourselves but have turned our eyes upward and have decided to love that person no matter the cost.

Just like Christ did for us.

By the time Peter wrote the letters we find in the Bible, his love for Jesus had clearly become *agape* love. He was a man totally sold out for Christ. Perhaps walking with his Savior and being empowered by the Holy Spirit enabled him to overcome whatever reservations remained in his human heart.

My guess is that Peter made the choice to love as Christ had asked him to and then trusted Jesus to supply the ability to do so. And perhaps what Jesus was really asking Peter that fateful day was not "Do you love me?" but "Do you choose to love me?"

He asks us this too. Do we choose to love Jesus beyond ourselves, to move past our own self-centered interests and even be willing to sacrifice our expectations? And, by asking us this, He also asks us to choose to love our husbands, to let go of our own agendas and interests and put what's at stake at the forefront of our concerns. He asks us to make the choice to love, no matter what.

When we are willing to sacrifice an easier path to be a part of whatever it takes to bring our husbands to faith, then and only then can we pray the most dangerous prayer.

Crossing a Threshold

*And who knows but that you have come to royal
position for such a time as this?*

ESTHER 4:14

It's birthed in the deepest recesses of our heart and then moves with our silent yearnings to a hidden place in our thoughts. We dare to consider the cost of what it may mean or require of us, until we finally submit and give voice to this most dangerous prayer:

Lord, do whatever it takes to bring my husband to Christ.

Among the unequally yoked there is an unspoken enormity to this prayer. We understand the journey it takes deep within ourselves to finally speak it—to pray it with sincerity, knowing full well that we have no idea what we may have unleashed. It comes from a place of near desperation and complete trust in God.

We are willing to risk it all.

At times the urgency of this prayer fills me with such desperation, I can hardly breathe. And when I am overcome by it, God tells me that this is just the minutest fraction of what He feels for my husband. Can you imagine?

Can you imagine a love that wild and all consuming? God feels that way about us, and He pursued us then just as He is pursuing our husband now. (Talk about really leaving a girl breathless!) This kind of love never fails. It's always there, protecting and watching. He's got our backs (see Isa. 58:8). We just have to trust Him and let go of our expectations, preconceived ideas, and fears. He will equip us to handle whatever comes. Can you believe that?

Amazingly, we'll find we are the ones changed the most by this prayer. At first, what we may have thought unfair now appears to be part of a grand plan. With each pruning, God strengthens our trust and reliance on Him. He shows us our fallen nature.

What are you willing to risk for your unbelieving husband to know Jesus? What are you willing to pray for him? Are you willing to walk into the unknown realm of God's will and trust Him completely with the outcome, no matter how you're affected in the process? It's a scary question to ponder.

When I worry what this prayer will cost me, I remind myself that God will equip me for whatever comes. That's been the whole point of this time of preparation (like John). Then I remember that God made the greatest sacrifice. He already paid the highest cost of all with His Son. And nothing I could lose can compare to that.

Prepared by God

During the days of Jesus' life on earth, he offered up prayers and peti-
tions with loud cries and tears to the one who could save him from death,
and he was heard because of his reverent submission. Although he was a
son, he learned obedience from what he suffered and, once made perfect,
he became the source of eternal salvation for all who obey him and was
designated by God to be high priest in the order of Melchizedek.

HEBREWS 5:7-10

From birth to death, Christ's life was a series of trials of preparation. Though we know few details of Jesus' life growing up, we
can reasonably conclude that God wouldn't have made His
Son's life easier than any other human's. Like us, Jesus learned
obedience and submission from His sufferings, as it says in Hebrews 5:8. Perhaps this represents the human side of His deity,
one so critical to His sacrifice being legitimized in a very human and broken state. We more easily identify and welcome
someone who knows and understands from experience our
own trials.

God prepared His Son for what lay ahead and equipped
Him for every step along the way to the cross. We can expect
the same preparation as His children and co-heirs with Christ.
Whether it's persevering through the storms in our life, meeting the challenge of a new calling or praying the most dangerous prayer to bring our husbands to Christ, God will equip and
prepare us just like He prepared Jesus.

In our life of trials, we can look to Jesus and see the pattern
of preparation. And perhaps therein lies our joy—in knowing
that God the Father loves us as much as He loves His Son and
is preparing us for the destiny He has planned for each of us.
And for our husbands.

There is an indescribable joy and sense of completeness in
looking back through past trials and realizing how God meant

every one for our good. He not only prepares us for the trials but also uses each one as training for the next.

In Ephesians 2:10, Paul says, "We are God's workmanship, created in Christ Jesus to do good works, which God prepared in advance for us to do." Ever heard the saying, "God never gives us more than we can handle"? That's because He prepares us. Trust in it; look for it. I promise you, it's there.

God wants us to walk forward in the trust and belief that He has prepared us or will prepare us for whatever comes. He's set everything in place to bring us through every trial we face. He's equipped each of us to walk the path of our spiritually mismatched marriage and to persevere no matter how long the journey may take—no matter how long we wind up waiting for our prayer to be answered.

Unanswered Prayers

Ask and it will be given to you; seek and you will find;
knock and the door will be opened to you.

MATTHEW 7:7

Unanswered prayers . . . what do we do about them? How do we change them to answered ones? Sometimes we wonder why God doesn't seem to hear or answer our prayers, whether they are for our husband's salvation, a stronghold in our lives, or something else that sits in our life day after day, seemingly unchanged. That may be how we feel, but it's far from the truth.

First, let's go to the root of the lie that God doesn't answer a prayer because He doesn't hear it or care about it. Psalm 17:6 tells us the opposite is true:

I am praying to you because I know you will answer, O God. Bend down and listen as I pray (*NLT*).

As a writer, I have a fascination with words, and their meaning and order have a tendency to capture my attention. The first part of this verse affirms the truth. The psalmist doesn't start with the request to be heard but first states the truth: he will not only be heard by God but will be answered as well.

Remember the story of Hagar? In Genesis 16, God hears her cries and even tells her to name her son Ishmael, which means "God hears" (see Gen. 16:11).

In the book of Exodus, God heard the grumblings of the Israelites over and over again. In fact, throughout the Bible, we see God repeatedly telling His people, "I have heard you."

So let's establish that, although it may seem as if God doesn't hear us, He *does*. Some may argue that unforgiven sin or habitual sins block this communication. That may be true of us hearing God, but I don't believe it incapacitates God's ability to hear us. We're the ones who clog the communication pipeline.

Now, with that established, let's explore our faith in terms of prayer. The act of prayer is also an act of faith. We believe God is good. First John 4:7-21 particularly speaks of God's love; namely that He loved us first. Let that soak in for a minute, because I believe it's critical to a Christian's ongoing faith walk. We must believe God loves us and always has our best interests at heart.

Not only that, but He also sees the big picture. He knows our past, our present and our future. He knows what we will face down the road, and He knows what we will need to do to actually get down to it. He knows and does all this not just for us, but for others as well.

If you haven't yet discovered how intertwined we are as the Body of Christ, you will one day, of that I have no doubt. Let me give you an example. Years ago, I wanted to start a women's ministry at my church with another person who I thought would be perfect for it. Yet when I prayed about it, God remained mysteriously silent. He had been pretty clear about starting this group, so why was He not saying anything now?

The answer came a few weeks later when this person who I had thought would be perfect to partner with turned from her faith and walked away from the church. How could I have missed that coming? Based on past and present interaction with this person, I thought the new ministry project would have been a done deal. But God knew the future. He knew what could happen. Yet until this person made her decision and chose her path (sadly), He could not tell me to move forward.

In other words, this situation wasn't just about me. Another person's decisions and choices played into the picture. To move sooner might have had tragic results. Instead of a ministry that's still thriving today, it could have been tarnished and could have failed.

I would like to present this question to you: Is it possible that God hasn't answered your prayer for your husband because He is accomplishing something else in him or your situation that is critical to how this prayer is to be answered? Is it possible He's doing this work not just in your husband, but in you as well?

So I ask you again: How do we change unanswered prayers to answered ones? Actually, we don't. However, if we change our thinking to believe that God hears and answers all prayers, and if we change our attitude from assuming defeat to expecting victory, then we choose to trust and wait for God to present His answer in His time.

The Perpetual State of Waiting

I wait for you, O Lord; you will answer, O Lord my God.

PSALM 38:15

If anything, we see throughout the Bible that God's people are often in some state of waiting. In fact, I've yet to meet someone who isn't in some sort of holding pattern. As Christians, aren't we all, in one form or another, waiting to one day meet Jesus?

We're all waiting for something. And I'm finding in this time of waiting that the most growth occurs, which seems like it would be the other way around.

Waiting is one of the most difficult places for us to be. We're impatient by nature. Waiting takes patience, which is hard to do in a world so focused on how fast something can be done. We're becoming a culture of impatient people. I see it in my own children. But I know from experience that waiting is critical in our walk with God.

But what's so amazing is that God waits too. Did you know that? Take a look at Isaiah 30:18:

> Yet the LORD longs to be gracious to you;
>> he rises to show you compassion.
> For the LORD is a God of justice.
>> Blessed are all who wait for him! (*NIV*).

> Therefore the LORD waits to be gracious to you,
>> and therefore he exalts himself to show mercy to you.
> For the LORD is a God of justice;
>> blessed are all those who wait for him (*ESV*).

I included the *English Standard Version*, which runs very close to the *King James* translation, because it uses the word "waits" instead of "longs." The original Hebrew word is *chakah*, which means to long, wait or tarry.

I don't profess to be a Bible scholar, but I found this most interesting. The root of *chakah* is related to the Hebrew word *chaqah*, which means carved or engraved in relation to piercing. Now take a look at Isaiah 49:16:

> See, I have engraved you on the palms of my hands.

The original Hebrew word for "engraved" is *chaqah*, the same word that's related to *chakah*, which means to long, wait or tarry.

I know this might be a stretch, but is it possible that God engraved us on His hands because He longs and waits for us and He waits for our unbelieving loved ones as well? I don't know about you, but to think that not only are we engraved upon God's hands but those He waits for are there as well just blows me away. Make a mental picture of your unbelieving spouse's name engraved upon the hand of God. And if I may make one more leap, I wonder if this engraving resembles the nail holes that pierced the hands of Christ—similar to the relation between *chakah* and *chaqah*. I hope that gives you chills like it did me.

But I have one final connection for you, and it's the biggest example we have of God waiting and longing: God sent His Son Jesus to us at just the right time. He didn't do it as soon as man fell from grace in the Garden of Eden. He didn't send the Messiah when the Israelites were captives in Egypt. No, He waited until the perfect moment in His timing, longing for us every step of the way with our names engraved on His hands.

God waited to send His Son. For you. For me. And for our unbelieving husbands.

Discovery

You know the saying "Save the best for last"? Sometimes the best can also be the hardest. Lynn and I understand how difficult it may be for you to pray this most dangerous prayer right now. Trust God to show you how to get there. He will, in His time. Pray along those lines before you answer the questions below.

1. Reflecting on the lives of John and Peter, what do you see as most significant in each man's mission? What doubts did each man have? What strengths?

2. Do you believe God is, can or will use you to reveal His Son to your husband?

3. What holds you back from praying the most dangerous prayer? What are you most afraid of? Make a list of your fears and bring them to God. Pray over each one and ask Him to show you the truth.

4. Reflect over past trials and look for ways God prepared you for them. How did each event change you and prepare you for the next trial? *Strengthen my faith in God, teach me patience & perseverance*

5. Read Romans 5:3-5. What keeps you from believing that God will prepare you to handle whatever is necessary to bring your husband to faith?

6. Pull out your list of unanswered prayers from chapter 4. For that third column, what are some possible reasons why it isn't time for each prayer to be answered yet? Write those reasons in that column.

Waiting can be the most difficult part of our faith. Using an online resource or a concordance, look up Scriptures that deal with waiting and hoping (for example, Gen. 49:18; Pss. 31:24; 37:7,9; 59:9; Lam. 3:25; Eph. 4:4; 1 Pet. 1:3; Heb. 10:23). Write down the ones that speak to you most on index cards (your favorite color, of course!) and memorize them.

Prayer

Lord, You are so amazing in Your love for me! I trust You with my life and I trust You with my husband. I give this precious man into Your hands and wait at Your feet for Your instructions on how I can be a part of Your plan for him. Lord, when I falter, help me look upward and remember that I am not responsible for the results. You ask for my obedience, which I willingly give You. Give me the strength and courage to pray this most dangerous prayer, and help me to trust You completely for the rest. Not my will, Lord, but Yours be done in the life of my precious husband. In Christ's holy name, amen.

Continuing the Journey

We pray that these 10 keys have begun to revolutionize your marriage and your faith. The journey that you're on is one that most certainly will have challenges, but don't stop learning how to apply these keys to all areas of your life and marriage. God wants to do an amazing work in your husband's life. We can think of no greater calling than to be a part of God's plan in helping him find his way to Christ.

Think of this book as a reference tool that you can use whenever you need a reminder or encouragement. And remember that God's Word is our greatest ally. Let the Holy Spirit continue to work in you, your marriage and your husband.

One final note worth mentioning is that if you are in a marriage where abuse and addiction have a foothold, we strongly encourage you to seek Christian counseling. God does not intend for us to stay in situations that are a threat to our safety. That does not mean God can't work to save and heal the marriage, but in cases like these, sometimes a temporary separation is the safest and best answer.

Our challenges in a spiritually mismatched marriage will continue, but with constant application of these 10 keys, you can thrive in your marriage and grow closer to the God who knows and loves you deeply. Make the commitment to walk with God on this journey and trust in His plan for your marriage. You will find that over time, your journey will get easier as you grow in confidence that God has your husband firmly in

His hand—as He does you and the rest of your family. Your calling is simply to love this man in your life and love God with all your heart, mind, soul and strength. Leave the rest to God.

Anything worth pursuing in this life takes time, work and, often, tears. Sometimes a lot of them. But God sees each one and will reward you for your faithfulness. He cares about every detail of your life, and He is working all things out for the good of those who love Him, who have been called according to His purpose. Remember, you are chosen for a high calling, and you have a front-row seat to watch the astonishing unfold. So, pull up that chair, my friend, and enjoy this crazy, challenging but fantastic journey. The best is yet to come, and it's all because of Jesus.

Keep your eyes on God, and get ready to experience His wild hope.

APPENDIX 1

What About the Kids?
(Lynn)

Train a child in the way he should go,
and when he is old he will not turn from it.
PROVERBS 22:6

I remember the first time I felt genuine fear about my daughter's salvation. She was only five years old. It was a hot summer day, and I sat in the kitchen with my husband. As I sipped my coffee that morning, I thought about how our baby girl, now five, would be starting kindergarten in a few months. In my mind, I had always assumed that we would send our daughter to the faith-based private school near our home. I made this assumption because up until then, my husband had been pleased with my decisions in regard to child care and rarely had anything to say about my choices in the matter. I bet you know where this is going.

I spoke over my steaming cup and casually broached the subject of registering our daughter at the private school. To my complete surprise, I was broadsided by an emotionally charged and unforeseen response.

"I don't want my daughter attending private school. I want her in public school." He stated flatly and firmly. Translation: She is not going to a religious school.

I lowered my cup. I can assure you, he was staring across the table at a woman who resembled a deer in headlights. I fidgeted with the tablecloth, trying to conceal my astonishment. His words hung thick in the air, firm and resolute. Shaken but not down for the count, I quickly gathered my wits and set out to help him see the error in his thinking. I laid out every conceivable benefit of private school. I conveniently omitted the spiritual element from the conversation. I saw no need to go down that path if I wanted to win this argument. I worked my position to convince him of the substantial value of a private education. After all, I was certain it was the best and obvious place to educate our girl. My true motive, of course, was my desire to give our daughter spiritual training, which I knew would rub him the wrong way. My logic was flawless, and I was certain he would cave in to my wishes after my clever and convincing reasoning.

He would have none of it.

The conversation ended. I relented, grudgingly; however, it was the right thing to do for our marriage. A few days later, the Lord brought "that" verse to my attention. You know the verse. It can make a wife cringe. Yes, the dreaded Ephesians 5:23 passage:

> For the husband is the head of the wife as Christ is the head of the church, his body, of which he is the Savior.

I had compromised. I didn't like it. Not one little bit. But the Lord truly knows what's best, and He reminded me that my obedience to His Word honors Him and opens a door for the Holy Spirit to work in my husband.

For weeks following this exchange, I couldn't shake my fear over my daughter's spiritual future. I worried if she would grow up to love Jesus. For the first time I contemplated the dreaded question that all believing parents who live in a mismatched home ask themselves, *Is it possible to raise children in a home where Daddy doesn't believe in Jesus? Will this home sacrifice my child's eternity?*

As a believer in Christ and as a mother, our thoughts and prayers for our children's eternity consume many hours. We fret over their future. We pray from a mother's earnest heart for our kids to know God. We beg the Lord to cement their salvation. And in the back of our minds, we are desperate to find a way to teach our kids about Christ as well as maintain peace in our marriage. It can appear to be an impossible mission.

Over the many years I have spent walking with the Lord, I have discovered a few truths. One of them is that it *is* possible to raise kids to believe in Jesus, even when Dad doesn't. You, as the believing parent, can help your children find and follow Jesus. These truths are trustworthy and doable, even in a spiritually mismatched home.

Where to Start

Love the Lord your God with all your heart and with all your soul and with all your mind and with all your strength.

MARK 12:30

The most powerful thing we can do to help our children love Jesus is to love Jesus ourselves. When we love Jesus with our entire heart, soul, mind and strength, we become contagious. In fact, that kind of love makes us irresistible.

When the love of God completely fills our hearts, it will seep out through ordinary daily life in subtle yet effective ways, thereby influencing our kids. I have found this to be particularly true with regard to menial events like cooking dinner, helping with homework, driving to a soccer game, to name a few. Our children possess an extremely watchful eye. They perceive more than we realize. They scrutinize our behavior and motives, determining if what Mom says Sunday morning, she lives out during the week. This can be a frightening thought or an empowering one.

Do you remember that in the second chapter of this book, I shared with you the most important time of my day? It is my daily appointment with the King. For years, I thought this early morning meeting with the Lord was just for me alone. However, a few years ago I discovered that my time alone with God has left a profound mark upon my daughter's life.

On any given morning, even now that she has grown to be a teenager, she will shuffle from her bedroom out to the family room where I sit in my robe, sipping strong coffee and reading my Bible. She ambles toward me, plops on the couch, leans against my side, pulls her cold feet under her and then gently rests her head on my shoulder. I subconsciously reach down and stroke her long hair. She is quiet and respectful as I read and pray.

She watches. She perceives.

To her way of thinking, sacrificing sleep to rise early every morning to meet with Jesus must mean I honestly love Him. It's that simple. She doesn't doubt my love for Christ, even when I lose my temper later in the day or when I fail to be patient or kind or even when I mumble "Idiot" when a car cuts me off on the freeway. Her faith is strengthened as she observes how I make the Lord a priority. Because my faith is real and prominent in my life, her faith has become real and vitally important in her life. My daily Bible reading and prayer time is a silent witness to my child. It has been the most powerful witness to the truth of Jesus Christ she will likely see.

You cannot impart what you do not possess. Our love for Jesus must be so contagious, so authentic, it can't help but rub off on our loved ones. When kids see us loving God in this way, they begin to love Him too. Don't worry so much that Dad is not a follower. Don't panic if he becomes hostile or even demands that the kids never attend church. You keep loving Jesus.

Teachable Moments

When I was a younger mom, I used to view the mundane task of driving my kids to school as a pain. I was working at a bank then, and it was a giant hassle to get through traffic, heading in the opposite direction of my office to take my son and daughter to school. Sheesh! However, after just a few short months of driving my son and then my daughter, I made a brilliant discovery. My car was a God opportunity. Sometimes my car was a prayer bus. Once in a while, it served as a confessional. Often our little isolated cab became a place where life lessons were received with an open heart and mind. It's amazing what can transpire when you have a captive audience. There's no escape from a moving car, and as it turns out, our prayer bus became a rich blessing in the life of our family.

Just this morning, as I drove my daughter to school, I reached over to the passenger seat where she sat, laid my hand on her knee and quickly prayed a spontaneous prayer over her day. These automobile prayers go something like this:

Lord, today let my girl have a great day. Give her something to laugh about, let her be a good friend, help her to remember her lessons and do well on the science test. Mostly, walk with her every minute of the day and protect her. Help her to remember that You are with her and when she feels scared or anxious, remind her to say a quick prayer to ask for Your help. In Jesus' name, amen.

This morning after I said, "Amen," she echoed, "Amen." She looked at me, I looked at her, and we smiled. All is right with the world. She gets it. Her faith is simple and it is solid, despite her daddy's skepticism.

These are the teachable moments of life. They often arrive at unexpected times and frequently they are never convenient. We have only a few minutes when our child is open to receive truths about living for God. So *grab* them. Take advantage of every teachable moment the Lord brings. Modeling prayer for my daughter while driving in the car may seem a bit zany. Nevertheless, it is one of those teachable moments that arrive with power.

I also find that the 10 minutes it takes to drive from the school after picking up my daughter in the afternoon is priceless time. I usually hear about what happened at school, her frustrations with teachers, or the pain of a friendship that ended. I listen and when she is finished getting it all out, I pray a silent and quick prayer, "Help me, Jesus, to say the right thing here." Then I relate a biblical truth and casually help her regain perspective. Mostly, I try to shed a sliver of hope onto her troubles. I don't spout off, "Well, the Bible says . . ." No, I share how her pain is understandable and how Jesus might look at the situation. What would He say about a friend who betrayed Him?

Decide today to be ready to stop what you are doing when these moments arrive and give your kids the truth. Our kids really want to know the hard truth. They honestly desire to understand more about their faith. They want to know if Jesus can really make a difference in their crazy and mixed-message world. They want to make our faith their faith, but they have questions and need to know the why of it all. I frequently ask the Lord to make me keenly aware and ready for when these moments arrive.

These often quirky and unexpected encounters with our kids pass in an instant but are profound moments that stick. My daughter will always have our prayer-bus conversations stored in her heart. They will guide her through her entire adult life. It's an amazing privilege to share Jesus this way with your child.

Start When They Are Young

It is true that in some spiritually mismatched homes, the very sight of a Bible in plain view is an invitation for a giant fight. I realize many of us face monumental struggles over our faith within our home. Maintaining peace with our spouse while also teaching our children about God can make us feel as if we are performing in a high-wire act. Every believer I know who is a parent desires to read Bible stories to their small children as they tuck them in at night. However, some of us might be in a place where our husband is adamantly against Bible reading. Take this pain to the Lord and ask Him to prepare a time in the future where you will be free to share from the Bible. Never give up hope. Our Lord *does* hear our heart prayers.

If reading the Bible is not a giant point of contention in your home, take time to tuck the kids in with a short story about Noah, David or Moses. A children's picture Bible works especially well with small children. Say a prayer together or listen to them pray before you turn out the light. Share with them the truths about Jesus and the gospel. Explain to them how life is better when we live according to God's plan. Make sharing God a comfortable and easy experience for your small ones. Make it fun.

As They Grow

On average (and this is a rough estimate), children spend 1 percent of their time at church, 16 percent at school, and 83 percent at home. We parents have such a great advantage, because we have them the most. This is true even in a home in which the parents are divided over faith. Don't waste your great fortune. Kids learn more from their parents than anyone else. They imitate and practice what we do, not what we say.

Our ability to influence our kids toward Christ will become more difficult as our kids get older and they grow into skeptical teenagers. At this point, they will no longer see Mom and Dad as the only source of advice when dealing with their problems. This is when the world begins to seep into their thinking.

I think back to that hot summer day when my little girl was approaching kindergarten. The fear I experienced that morning was somehow wrapped up in the future of my daughter's teenaged years. I knew then that she would one day wrestle with the reality of her father's unbelief. She would ask why. It was inevitable. I realized that at some point in the future, she would choose for herself to spend eternity in heaven or in hell. Would she embrace my faith and make it her own or would she reject it? Would she listen to Mom or to Dad? It's difficult for a child to process this dilemma. Kids are confused and conflicted when their parents aren't in agreement about faith.

Although the choice of whether to believe or not faces every teenager, whether the teen was raised in a two-parent believing home or a spiritually mismatched home, we still can coach our teens along the path of faith just as we helped them when they were small. The challenges, however, can be overwhelming and will often keep us on our knees.

The day will likely arrive when our teenager will no longer want to attend church. The argument often goes something like this: "Dad stays home from church, so why do I have to go? I want to stay home with Dad and watch football." Ouch!

It is nearly impossible to force a 16-year-old to attend church when Dad is home on the couch. However, until this day arrives, we must consistently encourage our kids to attend church, youth group, summer church camp or whatever program that promotes faith. Don't be overbearing, as I have seen this tactic backfire even within the home of two believing parents. Encourage, support, be understanding, fill yourself up with forgiveness when they disappoint you, pray down heaven upon them daily, and love them like Jesus.

I often scratch my head when I talk with women who live in spiritually mismatched marriages about the subject of attending church with their kids. I can't tell you how many complain that it's just too big of a hassle to get the kids up, get them fed, dress them and get them to church all by themselves. They lament how unfair it is and how Dad should help. I puzzle over their attitude that they would let an opportunity to bring God's Word into their children's life slip away because it's inconvenient.

If our spouse won't attend church, we need to go anyway and bring the kids for as long as possible. I know going alone is difficult. I have lived it, but I need to be there, you need to be there, and our children need to be there as well. We must help our kids plug into a source of godly influence. It won't replace the influence Dad could provide, but it can help tremendously.

So, what do we do when Dad objects to the idea of our kids attending church or, worse, outright forbids it? First, as I said earlier, don't panic. I know I panicked that hot summer morning as I contemplated my daughter starting kindergarten. I was upset, distraught and scared. Those feelings were a waste of my time. Our first calling is to listen to the Lord through His Word. We must respect our husband's wishes and pray every single day for his heart to change.

I have discovered that over time, and usually not more than a few years after a toddler is running around the house, Dad's adamant position against his kids attending church will soften. We can't let our anger and disappointment steal our love and respect for our husband from us. Continue to love him like Jesus, take advantage of every teachable moment, and never let go of the hope to one day have your husband's permission to take the kids to church. Look for moments when your husband is open to conversations about the kids and faith. That is the time to express your passionate desire to take the kids to church and respectfully ask for his permission to do so. One day you will be surprised when he turns and says, "Sure, go ahead."

Several days following the Kitchen Table Debacle, as I have come to call it, over sending our daughter to a private school, I sat down at a local restaurant for breakfast with a new friend. I had met Jenny the week before at our church Bible study. She was a tad bit older than I was and a lot wiser. She and I clicked from the start. I remember pouring out my fears about my daughter's salvation while Jenny listened. After she heard my story, she said something to me I will never forget. She gave me a Scripture verse:

> Train a child in the way he should go, and when he is old he will not turn from it (Prov. 22:6).

Jenny looked across the table, gently holding me in her eyes. She said, "Lynn, you do the best you can to train your daughter and then trust the Lord to keep His promise."

I cried. Tears of relief. Tears of hope.

She went on to say, "The key to this verse is the word 'old.'"

Immediately I felt a wave of peace wash over me. I knew exactly what she meant. Our kids may stray from living a life for God. They may outright rebel. They may buy into the lies of the enemy and embrace the ways of the world. They may choose to discount Jesus just like their dad has. It is a possibility, just as it is a possibility for children raised in a home with two believing parents. There are kids who choose to travel the painful path of the prodigal child.

But—and how I love it that with God in the story there is always a "but"—if we have trained our children, taken advantage of every teachable moment, encouraged them to attend church and loved on them with the infectious love of Jesus, they will return. I am proof of this truth!

Like Abraham, who believed God for a promise that was not fulfilled in his lifetime (see Gen. 12:2-3), we can also believe. Our child may return to his or her faith as a young adult. It's likely their faith will resurface when they begin to have their own children. It's funny how little ones will soften a heart. They may not turn back to God until they are 80, when they are "old." We may never witness their running home to the Father this side of heaven, but we can trust God to hear our prayers and pleadings for them. We can take God at His word. Our heart can rest in the security of His wild hope—the logic-defying, crazy, unpredictable and miraculous kind of hope we have because of the life of Jesus Christ. He loves our kids with a passion and commitment we can't begin to understand. And that's a promise!

Never doubt that God hears our prayers for our babies, teenagers and the ever-challenging prodigal adults. He listens when we share our concerns. Our earnest prayers move Him. He stores each shed tear in a bottle marked with our wayward child's name:

Put thou my tears into thy bottle: are they not in thy book? (Ps. 56:8, *KJV*).

As a mother and the only adult believer in our home, we have the privilege and responsibility to pray for our children. If we are not praying for them, who is? We must always remember that we have the ear of the King. We have His kind favor and His invitation to approach His throne to intercede in the lives of our kids. We have the privilege to bring them by name to the mercy seat of the Lord Almighty. We have grace to draw near to

God to ask Him to protect our children from evil people and evil spirits. To grant them perception and wisdom in a world filled with mixed messages and wicked lies. To ask for guidance and wisdom as they make decisions in their day. To plead for them to become men and women of grace, full of maturity, character, humility and integrity. And, most importantly, to ask God to move heaven and earth to draw them unto Himself forever. How awesome is that?

You and I will never be a perfect parent or a perfect example of righteous living, but we can be authentic. Love Jesus with all that you are. That kind of love is more influential than private school or an unbelieving dad or everything the world will throw at them. And that's a promise too.

Never doubt that your influence can help your children become followers of Jesus despite living in a spiritually mismatched home.

Prayer

Lord, my heart is full of hope for my children's future and eternity. I am calling upon You to intercede in my children's lives. Please protect them from evil people and evil spirits and grant them perception and wisdom to know the truth, Your truth, in their daily living. God, create in them a passion to pursue integrity. Teach them how to forgive, to be merciful, to have charity in their hearts and to love Christ with zeal. Do whatever it takes to draw them unto You, to discover the truths of Your Word and to live lives of authentic joy. Lord, I plead with You to lead them on the path of everlasting life, showing them how to be a man or woman after Your own heart. In the life-changing and powerful name of Jesus, amen.

Praying Scriptures

Praying Scriptures is one of the most powerful ways to unleash God's power into the life of our spouse, our family members and ourselves. The first section is a compilation of favorite Scripture prayers and testimonies from us and our blog readers. The next section is a wonderful list of Scriptures turned into prayers for the lost. The third section is for you—Scriptures of hope to pray to encourage and strengthen *you*.

Scripture Prayers from Us and from Our Blog Readers

For it is with your heart that you believe and are justified, and it is with your mouth that you confess and are saved (Rom. 10:10).

I (Lynn) pray this Scripture in Romans 10:10 every day for my husband.

He has made everything beautiful in its time. He has also set eternity in the hearts of men; yet they cannot fathom what God has done from beginning to end (Eccles. 3:11).

This is the Scripture God has called me (Dineen) to pray for my husband. I personalize it by praying, "Lord, You make everything beautiful in its time, and I know You are doing that in my husband's heart and life. You have set eternity in our hearts, and I ask that You awaken a yearning for Your eternity in my husband's heart."

> *For this reason I kneel before the Father, from whom his whole family in heaven and on earth derives its name. I pray that out of his glorious riches he may strengthen you, _____, with power through his Spirit in your inner being, so that Christ may dwell in your hearts through faith. And I pray that you, _____, being rooted and established in love, may have power, together with all the saints, to grasp how wide and long and high and deep is the love of Christ, and to know this love that surpasses knowledge—that you, _____, may be filled to the measure of all the fullness of God (Eph. 3:14-19).*

A woman who had been spiritually mismatched for more than 12 years prayed this for her husband every day. I (Dineen) have used it frequently since.

> *I keep asking that the God of our Lord Jesus Christ, the glorious Father, may give you, _____, the Spirit of wisdom and revelation, so that you, _____, may know him better. I pray also that the eyes of your heart may be enlightened in order that you, _____, may know the hope to which he has called you, the riches of his glorious inheritance in the saints, and his incomparably great power for us who believe (Eph. 1:17-19).*

This is a great prayer not only for our husbands but also for our loved ones, as are the following prayers from our readers.

> *Surely goodness and mercy shall follow him all the days of his life, and he shall dwell in the house of the Lord forever (Ps. 23:6). [Bridget]*

But blessed is the man who trusts in the LORD, whose confidence is in him. He will be like a tree planted by the water that sends out its roots by the stream. It does not fear when heat comes; its leaves are always green. It has no worries in a year of drought and never fails to bear fruit (Jer. 17:7-8). [Tracy]

Do not conform any longer to the pattern of this world, but be transformed by the renewing of your mind. Then you will be able to test and approve what God's will is—his good, pleasing and perfect will (Rom. 12:2). [Rosheeda]

Finally, _____, be strong in the Lord and in his mighty power. Put on the full armor of God so that you, _____, can take your stand against the devil's schemes. For our struggle is not against flesh and blood, but against the rulers, against the authorities, against the powers of this dark world and against the spiritual forces of evil in the heavenly realms. Therefore put on the full armor of God, so that when the day of evil comes, you, _____, may be able to stand your ground, and after you have done everything, to stand. Stand firm then, with the belt of truth buckled around your waist, with the breastplate of righteousness in place, and with your feet fitted with the readiness that comes from the gospel of peace. In addition to all this, take up the shield of faith, with which you, _____, can extinguish all the flaming arrows of the evil one. Take the helmet of salvation and the sword of the Spirit, which is the word of God. And pray in the Spirit on all occasions with all kinds of prayers and requests. With this in mind, be alert and always keep on praying for all the saints (Eph. 6:10-18). [Stacy]

For I know (perceive, have knowledge of, and am acquainted with) him Whom I have believed (adhered to and trusted in and

relied on), and I am (positively) persuaded that he is able to
guard and keep that which has been entrusted to me and which
I have committed (to him) until that day (2 Tim. 1:12, AMP).

I know this Scripture isn't talking about this, but I like to think that the Lord entrusted me with my husband . . . and as I commit him back to God, He will guard and keep him safe until he comes to the realization of the truth. [Karen]

And I tell you that you are Peter, and on this rock I will build
my church, and the gates of Hades will not overcome it (Matt.
16:18).

Lynn and Dineen, I am a wife of almost 34 years who has walked through a marriage road littered with explosive land mines, but because God is faithful, He and I were able to overcome my husband's drug/alcohol/pornography addictions, a long-term affair with another woman, and my husband's emotional, verbal and financial abuse and unrelenting controlling nature. *We* are now on the other side of this! And have been for several years now. My husband loves the Lord and spends much time in Bible study, seeking godly relationships in church and prayer. Our story is truly a miracle. Our four wonderful grown children have forgiven him and have a healthy relationship with him. I claimed many, many Scriptures through the years, but the one I still use and hold onto every day is based upon the principal of Matthew 16:18. The words are slightly different, but this is what I say and claim in Jesus' name: *"Upon the Lord I have built my life, my home, and my marriage and the gates of hell shall not prevail against it. Not this day."* God is sovereign, merciful and faithful, and it is only because of *Him* that I have a life being rebuilt on His foundation. He is truly restoring to us the years the locust ate away. [Cathy]

Scripture Prayers for the Lost

The following are Scripture prayers that you can use to plead for the salvation of lost people. Each prayer is based on Scripture and can help you offer powerful intercession for those who need the Lord Jesus Christ as their personal Lord and Savior.[1]

Father, in the name of Jesus, I plead that You will draw _____ to Jesus Christ in true faith and repentance (John 6:44).

In the name of Jesus, I ask You, Father, to quicken _____ who is dead in sins and trespasses (Eph. 2:1).

Father, I ask You to bind and remove Satan's work in _____'s life and to open _____'s eyes to the truth of the gospel (2 Cor. 4:4).

Holy Spirit, I pray that You would convince _____ that he/she is lost, separated from God, and headed to hell (Rom. 3:23).

Holy Spirit, in the name of Jesus, I pray that You would destroy any false ideas that _____ has about Jesus Christ and salvation through Him (Prov. 14:12).

Lord Jesus, I plead that You will seek out _____ and save him/her from his/her sins and eternal condemnation (Luke 19:10).

Father, I pray that You will open _____'s heart so that he/she will receive and believe the gospel (Acts 16:14).

Holy Spirit, I ask You through Your power and _____'s circumstances to prepare him/her to hear and receive the Word of God (Matt. 13:1-9,18-23).

Holy Spirit, I plead that _____ will understand the gospel when it is presented to him/her so that the devil cannot snatch it away (Matt. 13:5,9).

Holy Spirit, in the name of Jesus, I plead that the Word of God will take root in _____'s life and bring about true salvation in _____'s life (Matt. 13:6,20-21).

Father, I ask that the pleasures of this world and the pressures of life will not choke the Word of God that has been sown into _____'s life (Matt. 13:7,22).

Father, I plead that You will deliver _____ from the kingdom of darkness and place _____ into the kingdom of Your dear Son (Col. 1:13).

Father, I pray that _____ will receive the free gift of eternal life through Jesus Christ the Lord (Rom. 6:23).

Lord Jesus, I ask that _____ will not trust in himself/herself, but that _____ will completely trust in You as his/her Savior and Lord (Gal. 2:16).

Holy God, I pray that You would grant genuine repentance to _____, a repentance that will cause him/her to hate sin and to turn from it (Acts 11:8; Luke 13:1-3).

Lord God, I plead that You would grant _____ genuine faith, a faith that trusts in Jesus alone and surrenders to Him as Lord and Savior (Eph. 2:8-10).

Holy Spirit, I pray that You would stir _____ out of his/her indifference and complacency concerning his/her condition and his/her need of the Lord Jesus Christ (2 Cor. 6:2).

I ask in the name of Jesus Christ that _____ would surrender himself/herself to the Lord Jesus Christ (Rom. 14:9).

Father, I pray that You will send people continually into _____'s life who will share the gospel with him/her (Rom. 10:14).

Father, I plead in the name of Jesus that You will put a new heart in _____ and that You will place Your Holy Spirit in him/her (Jer. 42:30; Ezek. 11:19-20).

Holy Spirit, I pray that You will cause _____ to hate sin and that You will break the power of those sins that are hindering him/her from coming to Christ (Mark 9:43-47).

Lord Jesus, I ask that _____ would surrender to You, denying himself/herself, take up the Cross, and follow You (Luke 9:23).

Father, I plead that _____ will understand that his/her only hope for forgiveness and acceptance with You is through Jesus' work on the Cross (1 Cor. 1:18).

Father, I pray that _____ would not neglect the glorious salvation that is available through Your Son (Heb. 2:1-3).

Lord Jesus, I pray that _____ will feel and know the burden of his/her sin and will come to You for forgiveness and salvation (Matt. 11:28-30).

Father, I plead that _____ will make a genuine commitment to Jesus Christ as the Lord and Savior of his/her life (Luke 14:24-33).

Lord Jesus, I plead that _____ will not be content with the appearance of righteousness but will seek You for the transformation of his/her whole life (Matt. 23:27-29).

Father, I pray that _____ will see that his/her good works are as filthy rags in Your sight and that they will not save him/her (Isa. 64:6).

Father, I ask that _____ would believe and trust Your Son that You sent to be the Savior of sinners (John 5:24).

Lord Jesus, I ask that _____ would not die in his/her sins but would trust You and receive eternal life (John 8:24).

Because You came into the world to save sinners, I plead with You to save _____, who is a sinner and in need of Your grace and mercy (1 Tim. 1:13-16).

Holy Spirit, I pray that You would humble _____ so that he/she sees his/her need of Jesus Christ (Ps. 18:27; Prov. 8:13,29:23).

The "Six Questions" Method of Prayer Evangelism

Another way you can intercede for lost people is by praying through the following questions. These questions deal with the most basic issues of life. By praying for these items, the lost person can be prepared to hear and receive the gospel of Jesus Christ.

1. **Why:** Ask God to cause this person to wonder why they reject Jesus Christ and His salvation. Call on Him to show this person the foolishness of rejecting Christ and of living life without Him.

2. **What:** Ask God to cause the person to start asking the question, "What is the purpose of my life?" Plead with God to plant in his or her heart an urgency concerning this question.

3. **When:** Pray that God will grant this person an emptiness of heart. Ask God to show them that sin and selfishness will not satisfy. Call on God to cause this person to start asking the questions, "When will I really be free? When can I find true peace and hope?"

4. **Whom:** Pray that God will cause this person to doubt all the lies that he or she has concerning Christianity. Call on God to cause the person to ask, "Whom can I trust? In whom can I find hope?"

5. **How:** Plead that God will plant this question in the heart of the person, "How can I cope with my problems?" Pray that God will grant hopelessness in the heart of this person. Ask God to show this person that he or she cannot cope in his or her own power or strength. Pray that he or she will be forced to look to God.

6. **Where:** Call on God to cause this person to contemplate the question, "Where will I go when I die?"

Scripture Prayers for Yourself

Pray these Scriptures for yourself, or just read them and affirm that God is truly the wild-hope maker. Our greatest asset aside from our salvation is our hope. Keep it alive and strong so that the enemy's darts will bounce off your shield of faith.

But now, Lord, what do I look for? My hope is in you (Ps. 39:7).

Why are you downcast, O my soul? Why so disturbed within me? Put your hope in God, for I will yet praise him, my Savior and my God (Ps. 42:11).

Show me the path where I should walk, O LORD; point out the right road for me to follow. Lead me by your truth and teach me, for you are the God who saves me. All day long I put my hope in you (Ps. 25:4-5, NLT).

No one whose hope is in you will ever be put to shame (Ps. 25:3).

But the eyes of the Lord are on those who fear him, on those whose hope is in his unfailing love (Ps. 33:18).

Remember your promise to me, for it is my only hope (Ps. 119:49, NLT).

"For I know the plans I have for you," says the LORD. "They are plans for good and not for disaster, to give you a future and a hope" (Jer. 29:11, NLT).

And hope does not disappoint us, because God has poured out his love into our hearts by the Holy Spirit, whom he has given us (Rom. 5:5).

For everything that was written in the past was written to teach us, so that through endurance and the encouragement of the Scriptures we might have hope (Rom. 15:4).

Be strong and let your heart take courage, all you who wait for and hope for and expect the Lord! (Ps. 31:24, AMP).

Those who reverently and worshipfully fear You will see me and be glad, because I have hoped in Your word and tarried for it (Ps. 119:74, AMP).

But those who wait on the LORD will find new strength. They will soar high on wings like eagles. They will run and not grow weary. They will walk and not faint (Isa. 40:31, NLT).

Hope that is seen is no hope at all. Who hopes for what he already has? But if we hope for what we do not yet have, we wait for it patiently (Rom. 8:24-25).

Be joyful in hope, patient in affliction, faithful in prayer (Rom. 12:12).

May the God of hope fill you with all joy and peace as you trust in him, so that you may overflow with hope by the power of the Holy Spirit (Rom. 15:13).

Note

1. Special thanks to Dr. Kevin Meador and his team at Prayer Closet Ministries, Inc. for allowing us to share this list of Scriptures to pray and the "Six Questions" method of prayer evangelism; see http://www.prayerclosetministries.org/assets/PDF/Praying%20For%20the%20Lost.pdf.

Family Faith Record

(Dineen)

Only be careful, and watch yourselves closely so that you do not forget the things your eyes have seen or let them slip from your heart as long as you live. Teach them to your children and to their children after them.

DEUTERONOMY 4:9

One morning as I was driving to the airport to pick up my husband, I reflected on the previous day's excitement. My youngest daughter, just six at the time, had prayed with me to accept Jesus into her heart. As the importance of this life-altering moment in her young life struck me again, tears sprung to my eyes. I realized I couldn't share one of the most significant events in our daughter's life with my spouse. My heart broke.

I'm sure you've experienced your own heartbreak because of your faith differences. It's part of the ache of being spiritually mismatched. But one day I had an idea to help assuage that pain and prepare a gift for my husband down the road. I'd like to think that he would want to know about landmark faith events in our lives after he comes to faith.

A Family Faith Record is like a photo album with a focus. If you're a scrapbooker, I'm betting all kinds of ideas are floating around in that creative head of yours. Imagine pages filled with dates, journal entries, and even pictures of baptisms, lists of answered prayers and audio recordings of how God worked in amazing ways in the lives of your family. These are the events with eternal results your spouse can't see right now but one day will have the heart and mindset to understand.

If scrapbooking seems too overwhelming, simply keep a journal and write down the dates and events, as I do. Lynn uses a daily Bible in which she carefully records the date of each special event.

Imagine the gift you would be giving your spouse to show how you prayed for him and stood in the gap with Jesus during the time he didn't know Christ. The beauty of such a record is not just the gift of enlightenment but a permanent family faith history that will bless your children and grandchildren.

Be as casual or fancy as you'd like and start your Family Faith Record today. Keep a simple notebook where you note events and prayers along with significant papers and pictures tucked into the pages. Or go all out and create a full album with colored pages and photo images. Gather journal entries and include them, and embellish the album with stickers and pieces of memorabilia like the church program listing your child's name for a baptism or in a Christmas play.

A legacy of faith is the most important gift we will give to our family. Be creative and tuck away those priceless moments, not only for your spouse but also for generations to come.

Leader's Guide for Study Groups

The greatest among you will be your servant.
For whoever exalts himself will be humbled, and whoever
humbles himself will be exalted.
MATTHEW 23:11-12

Leading a small group is one of the most rewarding investments you will make for the kingdom of God. Thank you for giving your time, love and prayers to help others discover hope and healing for their marriages. Both of us thank you, and we have prayed, asking the Lord to bless you as you facilitate this study. Please tell us when your group will be meeting so that we can pray for you during your study (contact us through our website, http://www.spir ituallyunequalmarriage.com).

Helpful Hints Before You Begin

· Each week, greet the women as they arrive. Love on them. Make them feel welcome and comfortable.

· Listen more and talk less. Keep confidences. Encourage the women to share, and assure them that your meeting will be a safe place where they are free to be authentic.

· Encourage uplifting talk of husbands and let the women know that your group is not a place for husband bashing.

· Encourage each member of your group to speak. Although there are some individuals who can share easily, do not allow them to dominate a conversation. Steer the conversation to allow everyone a chance to contribute. Thank those who share frequently, and then ask someone who is quiet to share their thoughts.

· Always use the Bible as the basis for truth in your group. Allow for differences of opinion, and for the women to search out and provide Scriptures to support their opinions.

· Use your discernment, share your heart with authenticity, and allow yourself to be vulnerable without making the group uncomfortable.

· Be sensitive to your members' time. Begin the meeting on time and end it on time.

· Remind the women to silence their cellular phones.

· Invite the Holy Spirit into your group and expect the love of Christ to transform lives and marriages.

· If at any time you feel any of the members may be in a marriage where abuse or addiction is present, privately encourage her to seek professional Christian counseling.

· Have a box of tissues nearby.

Sessions

This is an 11-week study. After an introductory session, each week's study will consist of highlights from the chapter content and a review of the discovery questions.

The week leading up to your introductory session, cover your study and the women who will be attending with prayers of protection and a fresh anointing of the Holy Spirit. Call each participant, introduce yourself as the group leader, and remind each person of the meeting date and time and any other pertinent details. Let the participants know that you are praying for them. Share your excitement over what God has prepared for your group.

Any study that deals with intimate marriage issues will require discernment and sensitivity. Be aware that some women in your group struggle with the concept (or label) of being unequally yoked. Also, be aware that some women who join your group are married to a professed believer, but they are uncertain of his faith condition. Make each group member welcome regardless of their spouse's faith. Your group was hand selected by God, and you can expect Him to change lives.

Introductory Session

Consider having beverages available as well as nametags. Also have copies of the Member Class Form prepared to hand out and a supply of pens and pencils.

Welcome the women and get to know them as they arrive.

Begin with prayer.

Introduce yourself and share your story. Provide the group members with your name, phone number and email address.

Break the ice. Do something fun and easy. For example, have each woman choose an object from her purse and share how it signifies her life.

Review the schedule of the study: time, dates and other information such as a snack schedule if applicable.

Review the study format. Explain that as the group leader, you will highlight specifics from each chapter that are key concepts and the group will discuss them. Then you will review the study questions together and conclude with prayer.

Ask for prayer requests. An easy way to do this is to pass out index cards and have the women write out their requests. Have each person pass her card to her neighbor on the right, and direct that person to pray over that request for the week.

Remind the group why they are there: to study the Bible and grow in their relationship with Christ, to understand marriage according to God's design, and to learn how to be a vital participant in His plan.

Review the Small-Group Agreement, and then have each participant sign it and let them keep it as a reminder.

Have each participant complete the Member Class Form and turn it in to you.

Pass out the book and assign the reading of the first chapter and the discovery questions at the end of the chapter.

Time permitting, ask the participants what they are expecting to learn from this study.

Close with prayer.

Key #1: Know that You're Not Alone!

Welcome the women back with affection. Begin the session with prayer, inviting the Holy Spirit into your study group. Ask your members what impact praying for Jesus to be on the throne of their life is having in their life. Encourage them to continue praying for this for at least the next three weeks, if not longer. Offer an overview of the content. Review the questions and ask for volunteers to share their answers.

As this is the first session, be patient with the silence and be sensitive to the fact that the first week we tackle a difficult issue: loneliness in marriage. Encourage the women to share personal stories and guide the conversation to discuss how the women can find a community of support.

Assign reading and questions for next week, and close with prayer.

Key #2: Don't Save Your Husband—Save Yourself

Welcome returning members and any new members to your group. Begin the session with prayer. Ask the group members to share how they are keeping their appointment with the King and how that time with God impacts their life.

If you have ever spiritually ambushed your husband, share your story with the group and tell what the results were. Review the questions and ask volunteers to share their answers.

Ask a member to read aloud 1 Peter 3:1 before volunteers share their answer to question 4.

Assign reading and questions for next week, and close with prayer.

(*Suggestion*: If possible and financially feasible, schedule a date and time this week to meet as a group at a Christian bookstore. Look over the daily Bible selections for those who need a Bible and can afford to purchase one. You can also purchase daily Bibles through our website, spirituallyunequalmarriage.com.)

Key #3: Stay Connected

Begin the session with prayer.

Have a group member read 1 Corinthians 13:4-7 to the group and then begin the discussion and review of the questions. Ask members to share how they are intentional about staying connected to their spouse.

If possible, use a whiteboard or a large sheet of paper to list the qualities the group members appreciate about their husband. Leave the list up during the session. This is a great visual to further the impact of this chapter.

Be sensitive to the final sections of this chapter and allow the women to discuss challenges. Also encourage them to be intentional with regard to bedroom intimacy.

Assign reading and questions for next week, and close with prayer.

Key #4: Know the Essentials of Love: Hope, Joy, Peace and Trust (Oh, Yeah, and Respect)

Begin the session with prayer. Ask the group members how they're doing with the homework and encourage them to keep going.

During this session, ask the group members if they discovered areas where they need to respect their husbands more. If possible, and as they are comfortable in doing so, also encourage volunteers to share examples of unmet expectations in their marriage. Then explore how God can meet those needs in a much better and complete way. Ask if any of the women in the group are willing to share their list of unanswered prayers and if they found they had placed their hope in the wrong place. Celebrate each revelation as a new beginning to place their hope in God and bring more peace to their lives and marriages. Remind them that they will fill in the third column after they read chapter 10.

Assign reading and questions for next week and close with prayer. Ask one of the members to share the prayer she created from Ecclesiastes 3:11 and to pray for the husbands of the group members. Suggest the women either watch their wedding video or look through their wedding album in preparation for next week's lesson.

Key #5: Believe Your Marriage Is Blessed

Begin the session with prayer. Ask the group members if they were able to watch their wedding video or look at their wedding photos. Ask what memories or emotions this brought to mind.

Be especially sensitive during this session to any of the members who are still feeling shame because of their situation. This is a chance to help them walk out of this painful place and into God's freedom. Ask the members how they have been or want to be the aroma of Christ to their spouse.

Ask the members if they are starting to see how God is blessing their marriage and how their husband is a blessing as well. As the women are comfortable, have them share any trials they have gone through or are going through. Encourage them to share the good God brought or is bringing out of those circumstances.

Assign reading and questions for next week, and close with prayer. Point out study question 5 in chapter 6, and ask the members to plan something special—a date night, a love letter, a special meal—for their spouse before next week's meeting.

Key #6: Trade Perfection for Authenticity
Begin the session with prayer. Ask the group members what the outcome of their special plan with their spouse was. Ask if their husband reacted in unexpected ways.

As you review this chapter, pay particular attention to the section about sacrificial giving. Ask the members to share which areas spoke to them the loudest. Encourage the women to share ways they are working to communicate better with their spouses.

Assign reading and questions for next week, and close with prayer.

Key #7: Pick and Choose Your Battles
Begin the session with prayer. Ask the group members about their week.

During this session, discuss the words that create flash points of conflict in an unequally yoked marriage. Discuss what it means to "fight fair." Focus on the Scripture verses in this chapter. They are powerful and can transform a marriage.

Celebrate the changes you notice within the group. Perhaps schedule a lunch or a girls outing together this week.

Assign reading and questions for next week, and close with prayer.

Key #8: Move from Hurt to Healing—Seasons of Marriage

Begin the session with prayer. Ask the group members about their week.

Set the stage by bringing in some seasonal decorations for spring, summer, fall and/or winter. Start the session with a discussion of the seasons of marriage.

Review the questions and guide the group to discover areas of entitlements or expectation they need to release. Focus on the process of forgiveness and perhaps share how you have worked through an area of forgiveness within your own marriage.

This is also a session where the participants are encouraged to share moments or encounters in their marriage where God was present and active. Celebrate those moments.

Assign reading and questions for next week, and close with prayer.

Key #9: Keep Your Armor On—You're at War!

Begin the session with prayer. Ask the group members if they recognized any attacks from the enemy during the last week.

During this session, ask the members if they are becoming more intentional about "wearing their armor." Are they praying more for their husbands, for their family and for themselves against the enemy's attempts to discourage and bring turmoil?

Ask the women if they are building their prayer team and being intentional about asking for prayer when they need it. Also ask them if they are seeing a difference in their daily perseverance since they have started a daily quiet time to meet with God.

Assign reading and questions for next week, and close with prayer.

Key #10: Learn When to Pray the Most Dangerous Prayer

Begin the session with prayer. Ask the group members about their week and how they are trusting God more. Also ask them how their prayer team is developing.

During this session, ask the members how their perspective toward their marriage and their husbands is changing. Are they starting to understand the role God is calling them to play in their husbands' lives?

Ask the women if they would be interested in meeting once a month for encouragement and prayer.

Wrap up your study and encourage each woman to trust in Jesus and cling to the promise of 1 Peter 3:1. Remind them that they *can* win their husbands without words. Close with prayer.

Small-Group Agreement

I will pray to grow spiritually as an individual and as a group.
I will ask God to help me build a strong marriage through
the application of biblical truth.

I will give priority to the group meeting, arriving on time,
with reading and study questions completed.

I will pray regularly for group members

I will pray daily for my husband.

I will help the meeting be a safe place where women
are free to be authentic and develop trust and godly relationships.

I will keep confidences. What is said in the group will
stay in the group.

I will be patient with others, offering love and staying
clear of judgments.

I will feel free to invite other women to join the group who I think
would benefit from the study and prayer.

I will feel free to laugh, love and cry.

I will expect Jesus to show up.

Signed _____ Date_____

Member Class Form

Name _____

Address _____

Phone _____

Email _____

Spouse's name _____

Childrens' names and ages _____

What are you hoping to learn from this study?

_____

_____

_____

What is your greatest spiritual, physical or emotional challenge at this time?

_____

_____

_____

_____

How can your group leader pray for you throughout this study? What in particular would you like the leader to pray for?

_____

_____

_____

What questions do you have?

_____

_____

_____

_____

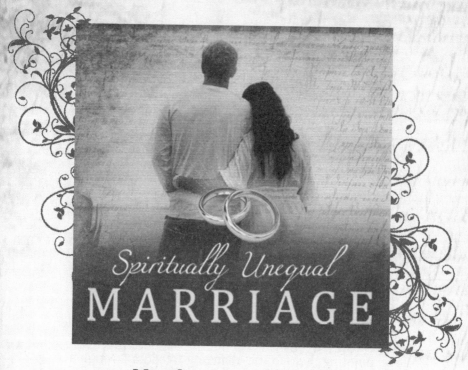

Spiritually Unequal
MARRIAGE

You're Not Alone

Since its inception in 2006, SpirituallyUnequalMarriage.com has become a valuable resource for individuals and churches. The site is filled with practical applications and encouragement to help spiritually mismatched couples thrive in marriage.

Lynn Donovan and Dineen Miller are dedicated to pointing others to God who is the wild hope giver in their unique marriage relationship. It is their passion to help others to discover this same hope for their mismatched marriage.

Join them daily and experience comfort and inspiration in a community that understands the challenges and joys of living unequally yoked.

www.SpirituallyUnequalMarriage.com
Facebook: Spiritually Unequal Marriage
Twitter: @sumarriage

Challenging Women to Live in Truth

Lynn Donovan
Author • Speaker

Apart from Me you can do nothing. — JOHN 15:5 (NIV)

A passionate writer and speaker, Lynn is a woman who presents a compelling message to encourage women to thrive in their marriage. She speaks at events nationwide where she challenges the myths women believe about love, pointing them to life-changing freedom through a relationship with Jesus. She reveals the zany yet meaningful stories of marriage challenges, truths, and triumphs in her life and invites women to share her view from her front row seat to an amazing journey; life lived for Christ.

She writes for Spiritually Unequal Marriage and is a contributor to the Internet Café Devotions and Laced With Grace, Devotions for Women. In addition to her writing and speaking ministry, Lynn leads Bible study and works in women's ministries at her church.

Married since 1992 to her best friend and biggest enthusiast, Mike, she lives in Temecula, California. They have a son, a daughter and a wacky dog named Peanut. She loves to laugh, enjoys a strong cup of coffee, Fantasy Football and not necessarily in that order.

She lives each day in awe of God's grace in her ordinary life.

Visit Lynn online at www.SpirituallyUnequalMarriage.com
E-mail: unequalmarriage@verizon.net
Facebook: Spiritually Unequal Marriage
Twitter: @sumarriage

Igniting the Soul

Dineen Miller
Author • Speaker

*And we know that in all
things God works for the
good of those who love
him, who have been called
according to his purpose.*
— ROMANS 8:28 (NIV)

Dineen readily admits that one of the greatest lessons
she's learning about life is that there's purpose in our
trials. And it's all about trusting God and putting our hope
in Him. Her favorite stories will always be of the miracles
God has wrought in the lives of her family.

Through this lens she also believes her years as a youth
counselor, a Stephen Minister, a women's ministry leader,
and a small group leader have prepared her for God's
calling on her life—to write for and speak to those in
mismatched marriages like hers.

In addition to writing for Spiritually Unequal Marriage,
Dineen writes for Laced with Grace and various other
fiction online magazines and newsletters. She's also
won several prestigious awards for her fiction, and her
devotional writing has been featured in *Our Journey* and
Christian Women Online Magazine.

Married for 23 years to a guy who keeps her young, she
lives in the Bay Area with her husband, two precious
daughters, and their dog Shasta, who no doubt is an
angel in disguise.

Visit Dineen online at www.SpirituallyUnequalMarriage.com
E-mail: dineen@dineenmiller.com
Facebook: Spiritually Unequal Marriage
Twitter: @sumarriage